Mediterranean Living

Designed by: Mark Vernon-Jones
Edited by: Christine Davis
Typeset in: Didot

First published in the United States in 1998 by
Watson-Guptill Publications, a division of
BPI Communications, Inc.,
1515 Broadway, NY 10036

First published in Great Britain in 1998
by George Weidenfeld & Nicolson

Library of Congress Cataloging-in-Publication Data
Lovatt-Smith, Lisa, 1967-
Mediterranean living / Lisa Lovatt-Smith.
p.   cm.
"First published in Great Britain in 1998 by
George Weidenfeld & Nicolson."--T.p. verso.
Includes bibliographical references.
ISBN 0-8230-2837-2
1. Interior decoration--Mediterranean Region.
2. Vacation homes--Mediterranean Region.
3. Celebrities--Homes and haunts--Mediterranean
Region. I. Title.
NK2195.V34L68 1998
728.7'2'091822--dc21   98-2702
                                          CIP

ISBN 0-8230-2837-2

Printed and bound in Italy

1 2 3 4 5 6 7 8 9 / 06 05 04 03 02 01 00 99 98

Mediterranean Living

LISA LOVATT-SMITH

WHITNEY LIBRARY OF DESIGN
An imprint of Watson-Guptill Publications/New York

contents

It cannot be entirely by chance that, after twelve years of vagabondage in northern Europe, I have come home, and am writing this book among the umbrella pines and honeysuckle of my native shores. I have a Celtic brew of sorts flowing in my veins but, as my mother used to delightedly embarrass me by informing all and sundry, I was 'made in Italy, born in Spain' – making me thoroughly Mediterranean, or so I like to think. While still in her belly I made my first journey, westwards across the Mediterranean following the same tracks as Ulysses when the goddess Circe bade him sail to the ends of the Homeric world, beyond the pillars of Hercules in the straits of Gibraltar. My blonde mother and I, not yet formed, left the Italian fishermen's port of Lerici behind us. Virginia Woolf described it prettily in her diary of 1933: 'A windy little town, of high pink and yellow southern houses, not much changed I suppose; very full of the breaking of the waves, very much open to the sea.' My mother has returned since for visits, eyes dense with memories, to the *trattorie* on the port. Accompanying her, and unencumbered with such personal

Introduction

The grand object of travelling is to see the

shores of the Mediterranean.

(Samuel Johnson, Diary, *11 April 1776)*

recollections, I was invaded by thoughts of Shelley's last trip and the poet's watery death. His house is marked by a small plaque and I pictured Mary looking out for him from its seafront balcony, forever waiting and watching tautly as the womenfolk of seafarers have no choice but to do. The Mediterranean fishermen of today still prefer the known dangers of rocks and currents to the unknown lurking in open expanses of water, and continue to sail hugging the coast as did the mariners of ancient times. On this little sea the weather can change quickly, at the mercy of its infamous winds: the sirocco, the tramontana and the mistral, among others. Like the peoples who live on its shores, it has blood on its conscience. From our sophisticated heights we may now consider the Mediterranean a mere landlocked lake, but it remains capricious, dangerous even, wrapped up in the same paradox as life itself: both nourishing the families that cluster on its shores and at the same time irrevocably fatal, killing at will. Even worse, the next wave can threaten with a new invasion, be it the Punic traders, the Greek colonizers, the Roman reformers, the Barbarians, the Byzantine resistance, the Islamic intruders, the crusaders or the contemporary tourist boom which has done more to alter the Mediterranean way of life in fifty years than war did in a thousand. But to return to the story of that particular crossing of mine. At the journey's end, my mother (of good northern stock) and I, unborn, were to find the same trees – cypress, palms, almonds – as on the Italian Riviera, and the same diet of olive oil and tomatoes, but the languor, the softness and charm of the Italians was replaced with the deeper passions of the Iberian peninsula. My first breath was thus – almost by accident and through maternal wanderlust – of the briny air of this great sea port from whence I write. Barcelona was thick with ambiguities, more so then than now. I was eager to be out in the open and appeared, impetuously, a month early following my mother's feasting on early strawberries and her dancing the night away in this air so soft and humid that the skin seems at one with it. My hungry lungs must have begun

That was definitely a feature of the Mediterranean –

the temples turned into churches, the churches into ruins,

the ruins buried until they became quarries for anyone

who wanted to built a hut.

(Paul Theroux, The Pillars of Hercules, *1995)*

A Mediterranean day is like a

dream whose effect persists after

its substance has been forgotten.

(Sean O'Faolain, A Summer in

Italy, *1949)*

Frustrated. Caged. These waves slopping dully landwards

have a sullen blue black look that constantly promises fury.

The sea. Its guts churn with flotsam and secret death.

(Naguib Mahfouz, Miramar, *1993)*

One can see the early adventurers, slipping on

from one inlet to the next, as we would turn the

corners of a road, in this landlocked sea.

(Freya Stark, Correspondence, *1927)*

I'd like to tell you how many million smells and sounds and

colours this place is, but my stock of superlatives would give out.

(Lawrence Durrell, Correspondence, *1935)*

to absorb the spirit of the place at once, all the thick atmosphere that I was to come to know so intimately. Just beyond the Hospital for the Foreign Colonies, where I made a considerable nuisance of myself for the first twenty-four hours of my existence, pimps and transvestites were plying their wares on the Ramblas, among the laughter in outdoor cafés, the love stories reflected in knife blades, the addicts still deep in the absinthe that Genet drank, the air heavy with the scent of deep-fried doughnuts. Beyond the port and up the Costa Brava was a world of fishermen, of onions being sliced and olives being crushed to make *ail i oli*. There were little donkeys labouring, and the first valiant tourists stripping off in coves with water that is ancient itself. Beyond the breakwater of Barcelona, across the sea to the east, there were the islands, the Corsican *maquis*, the murderous cliffs of Bonifacio, the sugar-cube villages eternally tumbling into the water. Further afield there was Rome, like a heart, still beating, but more slowly now than two thousand years ago. Southwards down that disputed coast,

mariners discussed eternal subjects, albeit under different guises: Scylla and Charybdis, *la fatalità*. Further still lay Greece – ready perhaps to rise again, Phoenix-like – and a million church bells, and glasses of burning ouzo. South were the swirling dervishes of Tunisia, the muezzin's call that paces the day, the ritual of the siesta, and all the million metaphors for peasant life and toil and pleasure. Here was the joy of mitigated temperatures, the slight swell of the waves on that deceptively calm water. All of this was mine in my first breath, sucked in with the humid night air. It has lead me to the irrefutable conviction that this timeless sea, its myths, religions and vices, connects its citizens more intimately than do race, creed or national allegiances. Or at least it should, despite present-day wars and genocide. There is a narrow strip of land that borders the Mediterranean, just before the wall of mountains and hills, large or small, purple or black, green or pure marble, that inevitably separates the coast from the hinterland the length of its shores. On this privileged ground we all eat the same things, are attached to the same rituals, live essentially the same life in the same kind of secular architecture. This sea, whose shores have hosted the main currents in civilization, creates its own homogeneous culture, endlessly absorbing newcomers and their ideas – and is the one I consider my own. I could swim before I could walk, long before people like us had swimming pools – why bother, with that immense blueness just a few steps down the unmade road? I was only conceived in the first place, my mother reliably informs me, thanks to the Italian recipes for ensuring fruitfulness for newlyweds – like most things hereabouts it involves large quantities of tomatoes. The *pomodoro* itself may only have been imported to these shores relatively recently, but it has come to epitomize the local cuisine. In the same way, I and some of the households in this book are not officially Mediterranean, but rather emotionally so. This being a land of traders and mariners, the new is always accepted and absorbed, becoming, in its own right, part of the dream.

… peace and happiness begin,

geographically, where garlic

is used in cooking.

(Marcel Boulestin, quoted

by Elizabeth David in

Mediterranean Cooking, *1950)*

One night the wind, like an

offering, brought them the smells

of apples, guitars, neckcloths,

donkeys, dust, mimosa, jonquil,

voices, garlic, desire. (Lawrence

Durrell, Panic Spring, *1937)*

Like a pebble on Ulysses' path, halfway between Sicily and Tunisia, the Isola di Pantelleria combines the ease of Italy with the allure of the Arab world; this tiny windswept island is a minuscule domain unto itself. We have no proof that the wandering Greek ever stopped here, of course, but if he had he would have found something akin in sheer remoteness to his 'Land of the Lotus-Eaters', latterly thought to be the Tunisian island of Djerba. But while Djerba is known as '*la douce*', Pantelleria offers little protection from the burning sun and the tricks of the Mediterranean winds. Here, suspended in a sea of endless blue, life has always been harsh. Homes have traditionally been at least partly troglodytic, niched into the volcanic rock in the manner of the Greek island of Santorini, and with some of the eye-catching drama of the latter's black cliffs. The landscape is rugged, and the local architecture unlike anything seen elsewhere. The houses, with their characteristic vaulted interiors, are known as *dammusi*. With their flat roofs (used for collecting rainwater) and numerous arches, there is a strong Moorish influence. Against all

I

odds, or indeed perhaps because of its isolation, the island has become something of a mecca for the chic *Milanese* crowd. It draws those who, like fashion designer Giorgio Armani, are obliged to go to the most remote corners of the world in order to 'get away from it all'. In Pantelleria, Armani feels free, unhassled – even if the fishermen's kids do congregate for his autograph in the evening when, tanned and sandy, he pulls into the little port after a day out on the blue. Armani's Mediterranean home consists of four low stone buildings in a dramatic garden etched out of the rock. Armani bought the land in the mid-1980s, when it was nothing more than a desolate stretch of scrub overlooking the sea, best known for its wild aloes and prickly pears. While deciding what to do with the site he lived in a small three-roomed cottage, without water or electricity. It was then that he realized that everything would have to be imported: the plants, the earth, even the water. It was obviously going to be a very big job so Armani commissioned Gabriella Giuntoli, an architect who has lived in Pantelleria for almost twenty years and who has been responsible for the design of about eighty houses on the island. Living here all year round, she is viscerally involved with the strange power of the place and instinctively understands what can and cannot be done within the island's indigenous building tradition. Armani's house is a luxury hideaway but has been projected with great simplicity, along the lines of a local village cluster. As well as the designer's personal suite the complex comprises self-contained guest quarters, connected by the rambling garden, a breathtaking salt-water swimming pool and wooden sun decks. The ensemble is majestically suspended over the sea, which can be reached by walking down 208 steps. The desert-like quality of the site has been revitalized with purely Mediterranean vegetation: olive trees, lavender, lemon rosemary, hibiscus, pomegranates and oleanders. In the evening Armani and his guests congregate for dinner in the main house, or on its terrace. Candlelit suppers in the scented garden are a magical affair, with the rounded roofs of the houses glowing through the trees. The magic may be man-made – the walls have been prettily aged by rubbing in substances such as red wine, while the ninety palm trees had to be shipped from Sicily by barge – but as the house and garden have matured, they seem to have become the most natural and pure expression of Armani's Mediterranean dream.

Giorgio Armani

On the opening pages: a portrait of Giorgio Armani and one of his frequent house guests, the actress Lauren Hutton; and a view of the unusual curved pool, from where swimmers can admire an uninterrupted sea vista. *Below:* a view of part of Armani's rambling home, which is made up of a series of one-storey cottages designed to evoke a local village cluster. *Opposite:* these outdoor cushions – for lounging or for sitting on – are covered with plaited dried vegetable fibres, an example of the work of local artisans.

On the previous double page: a breathtaking night view of the outside dining table on a summer evening. Armani delights in entertaining his friends and family in his signature generous but simple style, which echoes the tradition of the island where Arabic influences are ever-present. *Opposite:* the wind often blows very strongly on Pantelleria, here playing with the linen drapes that protect the terraces from the sun, hung around an outdoor 'salon' – again in the Arabic style. *Above:* a corner for reclining, by the pool.

Below: the kitchen is decorated with tiles in the local style but otherwise has a definite Milanese touch, being fitted out with sophisticated professional appliances. There is a whole wall of simple glass cupboards, and all the necessary utensils are at hand. *Opposite:* one of the bedrooms. The luxurious bed is shrouded in fine cotton fabric which doubles as protection from mosquitoes, an expression of Armani's talent to create luxury through simplicity. The bedside tables are local basket-work chests, and the walls have been coloured with a grey-green tinted plaster.

Pierre Cardin began his cataclysmic career at the age of fourteen, as an apprentice tailor in provincial St-Etienne. Then, as now, fashion meant Paris, so he took to his bicycle and headed for the capital. The war interrupted his journey and forced him to remain in Vichy France, where he perfected his techniques, but by 1944 he had made it to the big city. His ambition and clear-sightedness took him to Paquin, Schiaparelli and Dior in quick succession before he set up in a partnership making ballgowns for the flamboyant *soireés* of 1950s European society. By 1953 he had established himself on the faubourg St-Honoré. Here, with great perspicacity, he decided to launch his 'diffusion Cardin' collection – effectively the world's first ready-to-wear line. Over the next thirty years, all of the grand fashion houses were to follow his example. Cardin was the first to realize that couture was basically unworkable in the economic reality of post-war Europe, and that the future laid with licensees, boutiques and big-store collections. This pioneering democrat of the fashion world has continued his signature graphic shapes into the 1990s. Cardin's designs have

2

always reflected his own free-flowing curiosity, which has also led him to innovate in other fields. Some years ago, for example, he bought the famous Parisian restaurant Maxim's and later opened a branch in China, the first-ever Western restaurant there. Cardin sees himself as a promoter of the unusual. He is a builder, the archetypal 'renaissance man', a socialist thinker brought up in the humanist tradition, forever concerned with the world about him and perpetually on a mission to popularize culture. Finishing the visionary architectural folly known as the Palais Boulle, on the Côte d'Azur, has been another of his obsessions. The house was originally commissioned by a friend who died before its completion, and Cardin found himself bound to continue the extravagance to its rather splendourous conclusion. The house is a crowning point in the career of the Romanian architect Anti Llovag, who has dreamed up a series of interconnecting cells built without one straight line between them. Baths, beds, pool, tables, walls and windows – all are round or curved. Llovag delights in defying the traditional logic and mathematical rules of construction. Cardin calls him 'the most important architect of my generation' and delights in his sprawling mass of pink and peach igloos, of bubbles and space-age domed living-units that look as thought they have been made for moon walkers – all perched incongrouously, and breathtakingly, above the sea near Cannes. The twist of fate that twenty years ago brought Cardin and Anti Llovag together turned out to be fortuitous; the couturier's graphic aesthetic is reflected in this curvaceous palace. Although Cardin, with his Mao-collared jackets and black-and-white A-line dresses, has always tended towards a more angular approach, the two men undoubtedly have the same underlying visual vocabulary. Cardin considers the shapes of his home utterly feminine: breasts, bottoms and rounded tummies can be seen in its surreal silhouette. Cardin professes himself totally comfortable here; he sees it as a womb-palace, harking back perhaps to the ancient fertility goddesses that once were worshipped on the Mediterranean shores and who were later to find an echo in Aphrodite, born from the foam of the sea itself.

Pierre Cardin

On the opening pages: a portrait of Pierre Cardin, the maverick fashion designer; and the exterior of his Palais Boulle, perched high above the sea on the Côte d'Azur. Seen from afar the house looks like a bizarre space-age colony, with its clusters of cell-like rooms all massed together. *Opposite:* a poolside detail showing the globular windows in transparent plastic, echoing the space-age aesthetics of the house. *Above:* a view of the cascade which tumbles into the semicircular swimming pool. *Left:* the stone bench in the garden is also part of the structure, and curves its way around the lawn.

Opposite: a view of the dining area in the Palais Boulle, snugly set into a window. Cardin has selected the furniture – all of it contemporary – to fit in with the building's unusual proportions. Much of it was made especially for the house, as Cardin enjoys commissioning and promoting new talent in all areas of design. *Left:* the staircase, snaking sinuously up to the second floor, is created by an accumulation of cell-like units piled spectacularly on top of one another. *Below:* a stone-tiled bathroom, pure in its graphic expression, is set into the curved walls of the house.

Thought to be Ulysses' legendary 'Land of the Laestrygonians' – where the Greek adventurer was trapped by the canny islanders, lost all of his remaining men and was left to struggle through the rest of his misadventures on his own – Corsica has kept its reputation for fierce independence, reflected in its ruggedly mountainous terrain. Coastal settlements are few: the Corsicans have never been a seafaring people, and fishing has historically been only for domestic needs. Thus, the villages characteristically grew up on hilltops – where they were also safer from sea-borne marauders. Marie Chauveau was born in one of these Corsican villages; called Lumio or 'light', it perches close to the sun, high on a granite hill above the Bay of Calvi. As a teenager Chauveau left the village, as French country girls often do, to make her fortune in the big city. She went on to become a powerful Parisian-by-adoption and is now the driving force behind the highly successful style agency, Mafia. With her urban life encapsulating the exotic compendium of sophistication and stress that Paris offers its devotees, Chauveau's holidays and dreamtime are

3

especially important. This is when she escapes to her native island and the old house – inherited from her mother – that from its hill-top niche surveys the sea, the snow-capped mountains and the stone houses and red roofs of the mountain community. Crowning the village, the three-hundred-year-old structure is immediately recognizable as a typically Mediterranean dwelling, solid, distinguished and very proud. By buying up the two neighbouring properties Chauveau has been able to construct a rambling holiday home, all steps and walls at odd angles, with a terraced garden planted with cypresses and olive trees. Built directly into the living rock it could easily be French, Italian or Spanish – except that it is set among the *maquis*, the specifically Corsican undergrowth of tangled juniper, box, mastic, laurel and myrtle whose heady scent is the very breath of the Mediterranean. In renovating the properties, Chauveau's main battle was to convince local artisans to go back to traditional techniques such as applying limewash tinted with natural pigments and repairing old wooden window frames, after a whole generation of progress had converted them to commercial acrylic house paints and aluminium carpentry. She very much wanted to use age-old, thoroughly Mediterranean methods without sacrificing a modern approach. Her architect friend Colombe Stevens proved to be the perfect accomplice, understanding

Chauveau's need for colour, light and restful purity of line. Together they decided to keep all the endearing irregularities in the thick stone walls, the little stairways, the terracotta floors, beamed ceilings and oddly placed *œil-de-bœuf* windows. They then proceeded to design the interior along the lines of what might be termed 'sophisticated rustic minimalism'. This effect was created by allowing the internal architecture to speak very much for itself. The innovative use of flat applications of finely milled cement for the chimney-piece and the internal partitions gives a purity to the rooms that is somehow not far removed from the strong lines of the ancient house itself. Chauveau terms the experience 'a huge, adventurous undertaking in order to end up with something incredibily simple and beautiful'.

Marie Chauveau

On the opening pages: a portrait of Marie Chauveau in front of the Corsican holiday home inherited from her mother, which she has carefully restored over the last few years; and a detail of one of the oval windows set high into the wall, inspired by a window in the hay-loft of a neighbouring house. *Above:* a detail of the terrace table, set for an informal early autumn lunch. *Opposite:* the terrace table, made out of a piece of ancient wood placed on trestles. With its cane canopy, the terrace commands an impressive view of the village of Lumio and the mountains beyond.

On these pages: views of the sitting room and, right, the open-plan kitchen-dining room, the main spaces in the house. The floor was raised by one-and-a-half metres (five feet) so that two of the houses which were joined together to form the present house could connect, and a door was opened in the wall so that the sitting room could lead onto the terrace. The idea of using simple cement surfaces on the walls lends an air of modernity and simplicity to the interior that works suprisingly well with the seventeenth-century village architecture.

Opposite: In the shower room, the walls are of pure cement brushed with ship's varnish. The trough-shaped sink is also made of cement, and the taps are in copper. Towels are hung on a coat stand. In the bedroom, *above*, a cement panel serves both as the bathroom partition and a monolithic, brutalist headboard which centres the space. Reading lights have been incorporated into it. The table, in white-painted iron, is by design guru Andrée Putman but was sold through the cut-price mail order company Les Trois Suisses, an emblematic and forward-looking client of Chauveau's. *On the following double page:* another bedroom with great graphic impact showing innovative use of cement and natural pigments.

Writing about his beloved Corfu, Lawrence Durrell, surely the island's greatest literary advocate, enthused: 'You rise every morning to a new day, a new world, which has to be created from scratch. Each day is a brilliant improvization with full orchestra – the light on the sea, the foliage, the stabbing cypresses, the silver spindrift olives…' In his deliciously sensual travel book, *The Greek Islands*, he began with Corfu, premier among the Ionians, evoking its fantastically ancient roots. Did Anthony and Cleopatra banquet there before another of their tragic defeats? Did Shakespeare imagine Prospero's cave at the foot of a crystal cliff? Durrell was a connoisseur of the whole Mediterranean but it was Corfu, with its 'many million smells and sounds and colours', that cast its sensual spell most deeply and remained close to his heart. His writings evoke perfectly the atmosphere of the place, no less than when describing the Italianate buildings in Corfu town: 'Tall, spare Venetian houses with their eloquent mouldings have been left unpainted for centuries, so it seems. Ancient coats of paint and whitewash have been blotched and blurred by

4

successive winters, until now the overall result is a glorious wash-drawing thrown down upon a wet paper – everything running and fusing and exploding.' These words cannot but bring to mind the crumbling poetry of Piero Curcumelli Rodostamo's ancestral home near the village of Afra, in the middle of the island and twelve kilometres (seven-and-a-half miles) away from the main town. The house itself dates from 1750 and was designed by an Italian (indeed probably a Venetian) architect. The charming product of an eighteenth-century sensibility and the intensely rural traditions of the countryside, it is stuffed with the souvenirs of generations of discerning collectors. This is undoubtedly one of the island's most beautiful country estates, as well as its

largest, with an Italianate softness to it, amid the richness of the vegetation that characterizes the island's midriff. The Curcumellis originated in mainland Greece but during the long period of Ottoman supremacy moved to the Ionian island of Cephalonia, where the small village of Curcumelate remains as legacy of the family's stay. They then proceeded to Afra on Corfu, where Giovanni Curcumelli built this elegant residence on the ruins of an ancient monastery. The family has lived here ever since, surrounded by their venerable Venetian furniture, slowly decorating the place and collecting antiquities, icons, weapons and coins over the years. The house, of course, has crumbled since then and its large estates of olive groves and vineyards have been decimated by different inheritances. (The property has recently been designated a listed building by the Greek government.) Until her death a few years ago, at the grand age of 94, Piero's mother would sip five o'clock tea with her friends in the gilt-and-pastel salons under the watchful eye of a gallery of family portraits, some of which her son is now joyfully restoring. Piero's great-grand-father, Sir Demetrius Curcumelli KCMG, was Queen Victoria's Regent of the Ionian, and his memory is preserved by his great-grandson who still swims in that magnificent sea, hunts woodcock in winter and spends long evenings reading by the fire. No doubt the most illustrious of his ancestors used to delight in doing the same.

Piero Curcumelli Rodostamo

On the opening pages: a view of the façade, and a detail of the garden of Piero Curcumelli's home in Afra, Corfu. The house has been ravaged by time, and is slowly crumbling. *On these pages:* the drawing room. *Opposite:* The detail shows a wall hung with icons, and an English writing desk. Below is a portrait of Curcumelli's great-grandmother, painted by the Tsar's court painter in St Petersburg. *Above:* the two small chairs by the fireplace are nineteenth-century, probably French, and the piano is German. All these pieces are original to the house, and evoke its rather grand past.

Opposite: one of the two Venetian cabinets – both three hundred years old – around which the drawing room was decorated. It is flanked by portraits of Curcumelli's grandmother, and her mother. *Right:* a reflected view of one of the bedrooms; the twin brass beds were imported from England many years ago. *Below:* a view from the drawing room into a small sitting room decorated in a style evocative of the last century's fashion for chinoiserie; the chairs are Regency. On the near wall is a portrait of Curcumelli's grandfather.

Above: the gallery-like corridor which runs the length of the house on the first floor. As in most large Mediterranean houses, the ground floor would originally have been reserved for stables and storage rooms. *Right:* a detail of the stained-glass windows that punctuate the façade and cast warm glows of colour into the rooms. *Opposite:* the bathroom, with its decaying splendour. The armchair is colonial, while the plumbing is turn-of-the-century, but still functional.

Hugo Curletto is a flamboyant Argentinian who is Men's Editor for Spanish *GQ* magazine and a veteran of the fashion circus. He can often be spotted loping good-humouredly from fashion shoot to catwalk collection in capitals such as New York and Milan. His special turf, however, is Paris, where with easy-going, slightly grizzled charm and true Latin charisma, he is a fixture in that lively South American sub-culture that for generations has been part of the city's artistic soul. He has lived there, on and off, for the best part of three decades. He stands head and shoulders above his colleagues, not only because of his long, lean frame, which gives him a definite physical advantage, but also because of his utter unflappability. Curletto believes in enjoying life to the full and has long managed his schedule so that work is often combined with play; he does an enormous number of fashion shoots and much Aids-related charity work. His outlook on life is beautifully reflected in his rambling country house on the north-eastern coast of Spain. Situated an easy stroll from a small stone hill village, his house is a traditional Catalan *masia*, hard by the desirably

5

chic seaside resorts of Cadaques and Bagur. You will often find Curletto sitting with his feet in the sand, in one of the small deserted coves that constitute the great charm of the Costa Brava out of season, refuelling on freshly caught shellfish before another smooth transition into jet-setting journalism. He loves this rocky coast with a passion – its transparent waters and jutting inlets, its grey rock and scented pine woods, the field of sunflowers below his house, the unspoilt valley behind it. He likes the friendliness of the people, the easy rhythm of life here where tourists are strictly a seasonal occurrence. Most of all, he loves the sprawling stone mass of the rural farm itself. Seldom has a house so well reflected its owner. South-facing, big and rangy, informally elegant, slightly shabby but visually arresting, it has been furnished slowly by Curletto over the years. He has transformed it from a roofless 'island of grey stone among the sunflowers' into a home, where he has respected the distinctive layout of the Catalan *masias* that originated in the seventh century. Upon entering via the original studded wooden double doors, one is faced with a huge windowless room (which previously housed livestock) around which the other rooms are set. This layout is repeated on the first floor and reflects a very ancient Mediterranean blueprint, hailing back to Roman times. Curletto's *masia* was probably built during the seventeenth century, a time of great prosperity in the region. With its vast spaces it is perfect for entertaining floods of friends, and is particularly comfortable because of the abundance of largish, terracotta-flagged bedrooms around the spacious common areas. The ancient floor plan has thus turned out to be ideal for the easy, informal living that Curletto prefers, so apart from new bathrooms and enlarged windows, the house has remained essentially true to itself. The *masia*'s decorative impact is subtle, stemming from the pale washes of colour on the walls. Curletto has given each room a prevalent colour or theme, and anchored them with huge pieces of furniture, often of simple workmanship but with a certain rural elegance. Wood, stone and the local La Bisbal ceramics, which he delights in, are now, as then, the favoured decorative materials. Curletto has been wise in largely leaving his farm unadorned. Its intrinsic austerity is well balanced with his poetic use of colour and his artist's eye for arrangement.

Hugo Curletto

On the opening pages: a portrait of Hugo Curletto, and two views of the garden façade of his *masia* in the Baix Ampurdan. *Right:* a general view of the large hall, which traditionally lies at the heart of this type of rural Catalan construction. The bench, *above,* was in the house when Curletto bought it; it is a classic example of what would have been the main piece of furniture in the room. The hats have all been brought back from South America during Curletto's extensive travels around his native continent. *Opposite:* detail showing a view from the main hall into the kitchen and the chromatic variations in the purposely peeling and faded paintwork. The door is a leaf of the original entrance door and is probably over two hundred years old.

Opposite: views of the first-floor hallway, which echoes the scale and proportions of the main hall below. The stairway behind the wall (seen in the top picture) leads to the roof terrace. The table is rural Spanish Baroque. The details show a pair of ancient chests which were found in the house, and two paintings from Curletto's vast collection. The one on the left, of a celebrated torero, is actually a black-and-white photograph which has been painted. *Left:* a desk, thought to come from one of the local spa hotels, and a Catalan Art Deco office chair. *Below:* the guest bedroom, known as the Spanish Room, decorated with framed pages from *El Lidia*, a magazine that featured portraits of toreros in the 1940s. The bed is turn-of-the-century and was bought locally.

Above: a view of the Yellow Room, a guest room that gives onto
the façade above the front door. The plaster shelf is original to
the house and was used for hanging clothes. The bed is local,
bought at one of Barcelona's *encantes* or flea markets, and
boasts a pretty inlaid medallion. The chair, one of a set, is a
simple 1930s design. *Opposite:* details of the Yellow Room and
the bathroom, which was designed by Curletto to evoke the
spacious and minimalist bathrooms of the Art Deco period.
The ceramic tiles are all local, bought at the nearby potters'
town of La Bisbal. The column is in green marble powder
applied onto cement.

Below: the rose-coloured kitchen, with its traditional arched ceiling. Curletto has an extensive collection of cheerful multi-coloured French pottery from the immediate post-war period, which he has been buying at Paris flea markets for years. The chairs are sturdy rustic pieces with straw seats. The detail shows three large serving plates from the local potters' kilns at La Bisbal. *Opposite:* a corner of the lounge with a high bench, also made locally, covered with pink mattress ticking. The lamp was made by Curletto from a 1940s fragment of wrought iron. *On the following double page:* a view of the sumptuous terrace, overgrown with climbing roses. The iced mint tea dispenser was bought from a water-seller on a trip to Istanbul.

The painter Timothy Hennessy lives in an ancient house in a singularly beautiful little port, the quintessence of Mediterranean romanticism. Knowingly, he has no telephone but to contact him three words on an envelope suffice: Hennessy, Hydra, Greece. Since 1957 this volcanic Greek island has been one of the emotional anchors in Hennessy's busy transcontinental life. Hydra was once a fabulously wealthy base for trade and piracy. From the seventeenth century onwards, successful corsairs and merchants built themselves great houses by tunnelling into the volcanic rock. Some of these were self-contained mansions with their own cisterns, bakeries and sheltered women's quarters as well as terraced gardens and patios. A number of these graceful residences survive to this day. When Hennessy first came to Hydra – on a visit to the local painter Ghika – he was immediately smitten and bought a magnificent ruin for $2,000. The home Hennessy has subsequently created, over the last forty years, reflects the sophistication of his taste and his cosmopolitan background. The interior is crammed with various collections and beloved bits and pieces acquired

6

over the years. Traces can be seen of his American birth and his upbringing in St Louis, Missouri, the Frenchified southern capital that would have been founded by his ancestors about the same time that his future home on Hydra was beginning to be built. Then came other influences: an artistic training at the studio of André Lohte in his ancestral France, and two formative years in the buzzing atmosphere of St-Germain-des-Prés in the early 1950s; then time spent in Italy and an aristocratic first marriage, which involved Hennessy in the decadence of Venetian social splendour; later came wanderings with his second wife Isabelle and their son Sebastian between exquisite residences in Eire, Venice and Paris. But it is to Hydra that he has always returned, content here even in the heat of the summer when the little port retains the fury of the sun. The house Hennessy has created is like a living work of art, its walls lined with his own abstract geometrical paintings on un-stretched and unframed canvases. Family heirlooms jostle with antiquities on the shelves, and a certain grace in the arrangements of the objects evokes a *Gone with the Wind*-style Deep South, the gallery of a noble Irish manor, or the drawing room of his grand great-aunt Mimi, with whom he lived as a child and who gave him his first taste of art. As an artist, Hennessey embraces many disciplines, from the Fortuny-style painted dresses he created in the 1970s to collage, performance art and fresco – an example of the latter can be seen in the salon on the second floor. His home is gloriously littered with this effusive art, which is both intristic to the surrounding space and reflects the constant inspiration of the sea beneath the terrace. Here, arches frame the little port, all white and Cubist, that tumbles like spilt sugar cubes down to the timeless sea that feeds it.

Timothy Hennessy

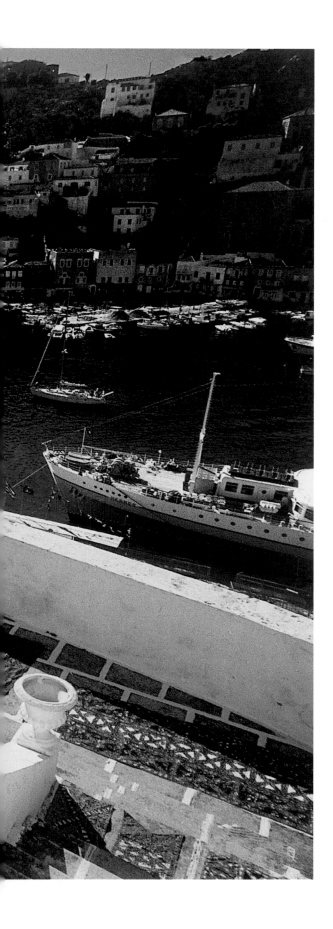

On the opening pages: a portrait of Timothy Hennessy at work on his terrace, and a view of the façade of his house from the port. Over the years Hennessy has painstakingly restored the three-hundred-year-old structure. *Left:* Hennessy's double-sided paintings are laid out on the terrace, with the stunning view forming a permanent backdrop. His art is always thus incorporated into the fabric of the house and into its Mediterranean context. *Top:* on the walled terrace is an evocative arrangement of urns and sculpture around a niche, which might originally have housed a saint. *Above:* in the sunken patio, chairs and tables painted by Hennessy sit under the luxuriant climbing plants entwined on the pergola.

Opposite: The winter drawing room, where the sun streaks in all year round. Hennessy is not interested in decoration as such but rather in the impact of the house as a whole, within its natural context. Art, architecture and furnishings have all been designed to this effect. The brass chandelier was found in northern Greece, and the neo-Renaissance table was painted by Hennessy. *On this page:* details of the house showing the pivotal position that the painter's canvases occupy in the space, juxtaposed with fine antiques of diverse origin.

Right: the ground floor. Being moulded into the rock itself, and with its high ceilings, this level is mainly used in summer. The port of Hydra is known as one of the hottest in the Greek islands due to its position as a natural harbour, sheltered from the wind. The ancient houses, set into the volcanic rock, were designed to catch every breeze and to be kept dark for coolness. Here the furniture includes turn-of-the-century English chairs and a late eighteenth-century table, also English. The soup tureen is faience, from Italy.

The origins of this house lie with the Bauhaus philosophy absorbed by Peter Klasen when he was at art school in Berlin. The results, however, are plainly Mediterranean. The four buildings, set out on a breathtaking site near Grasse in the south of France, are designed for outdoor living. The flat roofs, patios and terraces, and most importantly the ingenious use of different openings to maximize the quality of the light, have their roots in age-old techniques. Klasen is one of the most representative artists of the *nouvelle figuration* in France, and is collected by many museums. The Klasens are based in Paris but spend about three-and-a-half months a year in Châteauneuf-de-Grasse. Here, in the wooded hills behind Cannes, the easy-going attitude of the south permeates their way of life. This is a relatively unspoilt area, with villages that cling to the sides of the hills and where flowers are still grown for perfume-making – which has been an industry here for centuries. Klasen takes pleasure in working in such a profoundly stimulating environment. He manages this, despite the constant parade of impromptu visitors, dealers, critics and children,

7

since the compound has separate buildings for the main living space, the staff quarters, a visitors' cottage and the atelier. In this huge, light-drenched studio, with its cathedral ceilings that soar to a height of eight metres (twenty-six feet), Klasen explores techniques that the narrower confines of his Paris workspace and schedule would not allow. He credits the house with his debuts in sculpture, for instance, and also for stimulating his interest in ceramics, due to the large number of local pottery kilns. For the minimalist façade of the house he created his own modern bas-reliefs at a ceramic workshop in the nearby village of Opio. The Klasens had long been fond of the area. In the mid-1970s they had a house in nearby Tourettes-sur-Loup, a picturesque town famous for its violets, where they made the acquaintance of an architect neighbour, Christopher Petitcollot. Klasen was struck by the fact that although Petitcollot had built in the surrounding countryside, none of the finished projects seemed to express the radical modernity of the architect's vision. Strict local planning laws – and a lack of truly adventurous clients – have meant that innovative contemporary constructions are few and far between, despite the Côte d'Azur's tradition of inventive architecture. Evoking not only the Bauhaus but also Frank Lloyd Wright and Richard Meier, the two men began 'to dream of a unique house, reduced to its essential, based on the concepts of clarity and transparency'. With their joint vision confirmed, the hunt began for a suitable site, a laborious process that took almost as long as did the subsequent building. Once this piece of land was located the owners then had to be persuaded to sell. This they apparently had no intention of doing. Caught up in the painter's enthusiasm for the project, however, they eventually relented. Thus, from the beginning, the creation of the house was what Klasen terms *'une histoire heureuse'*. Once the plans were completed, in 1990, there began what the painter calls a 'symbiotic relationship with Petitcollot – a deep friendship and mutual understanding that was not tried by the experience of constructing something, but rather strengthened and added to'. This affinity was to serve them well, as Petitcollot was able to carry out his most significant commission and Klasen, after two-and-a-half years of building, was able to move his baby daughter, Joy, straight into the new house, for her first Mediterranean summer.

Claudine &
Peter Klasen

On the opening pages: a portrait of the artist Peter Klasen by his
wife, the photographer Claudine D'Hellemmes; and a view of
the artist's studio, housed in its own building, with floor-to-
ceiling windows and a spectacular view of the Curoumettes
hills beyond. *Opposite:* a view of the courtyard façade of the
main house. The kitchen gives onto this courtyard, as do the
windows of the bedrooms on the top floor. The white of the
façade comes from the external plastering, made with the
characteristically pale sand of the local Provençal village of
Biot. *Above:* the roof terrace, with its vintage chairs.

Opposite: a view of the open-plan living space in the main house, as seen from the mezzanine. The ray of sunlight comes from a slit in the roof designed to give just that effect. The room contains several of Klasen's paintings, and a few pieces from his collection of African statues. *Below:* another view of the same room, here showing the adjacent dining room where the chairs are all assorted pairs by designers such as Starck, Prouvé and Eames. The sofa in the foreground was designed by Claudine. *Left:* the entrance, showing a Dogon stair-sculpture and Kirdi shield hung opposite a Klasen painting.

As many an exhausted friend will testify, Nadia and Suomi La Valle are effervescent, energetic and enormous fun. Suomi is half-Finnish and half-Italian – a curious mix – and Nadia is Milanese. They met, rather glamorously, at the restaurant of the Cipriani in Asolo, near Venice, when Nadia was a house guest of the philanthropist Evelyn Lambert. Asolo remains 'home', although they have travelled the world and are equally at ease in London as in Italy or, latterly, Morocco. The pair are utterly different in character, but complement each other perfectly. She is a clothes designer with an array of fashionable clients; he an eclectic photographer whose poetic visual essay, a one-off volume called *Hashish*, is a collector's item. Suomi has not been too bothered about finding a more commercial application for his picture-making talents, however, since he has lately been focused in another direction: the restoration and revamping of a small Moorish palace in the heart of Tangiers. What for others would have been the project of a lifetime, for the La Valles was more of a passionate aside in a life overflowing with movement. The couple first hit the city,

8

strategically situated on the cusp of the Mediterranean, in the late 1980s. With its piecemeal history, its connotations of irreverent decadence, its busy port, its artistic expats and its humid summers, Tangiers can either seduce or repel. It is a city of mixed blood and mixed metaphors. The La Valles loved it at once, its sense of mysterious sophistication suiting them perfectly, and they spent several summers here. One day, rather on the spur of the moment, they decided it would be fun to look into buying a house. The evening before they were due to leave they found themselves visiting a good, solid 1850s town house behind the American Legation, very near the *Socco Chico*, in the depths of the medina. Today, curled up on the brocade sofa, they laugh at the memory: 'We didn't even have to look at each other… we knew we had to have it.' Nadia subsequently named the house *Dar Maktoub* – 'it is written'. The restoration was a long and hazardous affair, done with the help of Abdelaziz, the La Valles' right-hand man, who took up residence from the day they signed the deeds. It was to be four long years, however, before the couple could move in themselves. What appeared to be an unassuming Moroccan house, or *dar* – with rooms and salons arranged in traditional style around a columned courtyard and crowned by a multi-level roof terrace – turned out to be full of surprises. Suomi chanced upon a Roman well and some 1920s additions, and discovered an annexe containing a long-abandoned synagogue from when the house belonged to a prominent Jewish family. Indeed, the building is situated near the rue des Bijoutiers, the former goldsmiths' quarter and an area which would once have been predominantly Jewish. The ruined synagogue has now been converted by Suomi into a southern version of a cedar-beamed baronial hall, with the aid of some striking stained glass salvaged from the ruins of Tangiers' French cathedral. He also designed and made the monumental fireplace, which adds to the medieval effect. The whole house was completely redecorated using *tadlakt*, an ancient technique for producing an effect somewhat like *stucco Veneziano* on the walls. In fact living in Tangiers, say the La Valles, has the same timeless quality that living in Venice has – except of course for the summer heat and the regular cry of the muezzins pacing the day.

Nadia & Suomi La Valle

On the opening pages: a portrait of Nadia La Valle by her daughter Evi-Elli. She stands in her Tangiers kitchen surrounded by some of the five thousand roses that her husband gave her for her fiftieth birthday, which she celebrated with a big party in Dar Maktoub. Opposite is a view from the roof terrace towards the port. The tent, for al fresco tea parties and dining, was specially made in the souk. The cushions on the smaller terrace come from Fez and are in hand-woven brocade. *Opposite:* the main guest-room with its ornate iron bedstead. *Above:* the courtyard, the heart of the house from which most of the other rooms lead off, with its original black and white marble floor and 1930s *marmorino* columns.

Above: an ornate salon with an original mosaic floor and walls in the local stucco technique, known as *tadlak*. Like the rest of the house this room was entirely restored and then decorated by Suomi La Valle. *Opposite:* the dining room, once a synagogue, with its high ceilings and large structural beams in cedar wood. The stained glass windows originally belonged to the French cathedral in Tangiers. The chimney was designed and painstakingly constructed by Suomi La Valle. Its columns are in *bianco latte* marble, imported from Carrara. Practical during the short but damp winter, the chimney also adds to the 'baronial hall' effect of the large rectangular room.

On the opening pages: Jean-Pierre and Zeïneb Marcie-Rivière's Japanese spaniel, Gandi, and the front door of the house, a nineteenth-century piece bought in the souks of Tunis. *On these pages:* views of the various courtyards showing, above, the original water reservoirs; opposite top, the table set for lunch (the mosaic in the background is a copy of one in the museum at Carthage); opposite, the entrance to the small house where the main living quarters are situated; right, the door of what used to be the local café and is now a highly unusual living room.

On the previous double page: the Café Maure has been restored and simply decorated with local-style rush matting, and is now used as a sitting room. Clients, all men, would once have sat crossed-legged on the four raised platforms, sipping tea and smoking the *narguile* (hookah). *Above:* a hallway featuring woodwork by the local carpenter and a tiled floor inspired by local Roman remains. The bench, inlayed with mother of pearl, is of Syrian origin, bought in Tunis. *Left:* Tunisian pottery and painting. *Opposite:* a bedroom, with the characteristic local wrought-iron window screens and a Tunisian boxed bed in painted wood. The side table is turn-of-the-century, and the floor combines marble with ceramic tiles.

David Massey is well known as a photographer in the grand old *Vogue* tradition. It was that magazine's famed art director, Alexander Libermann, who in the early 1960s advised him to specialize in interiors. This type of photography gave Massey a pretext to travel widely and allowed him a privileged perspective on what the French call *les arts de vivre*. Massey now enjoys a life of leisure, dividing his time between his seventeenth-century apartment in the Place des Vosges in Paris and his Tunisian home. It was back in 1967 that Massey and his companion, the painter Gaston Berthelot, decided to build a house here. As a man of refined aesthetic sensibilities Massey felt a strong compulsion to build a place of his own; moreover, he was fed up with the ravages that tourism had brought to Italy and the south of France. The location they chose was Hammamet, on the Mediterranean shores. If it sounds exotic today, it was even more so in the 1960s when Tunisia was relatively undiscovered. With its beautiful old walled medina and the transparent, emerald sea nearby, Hammamet has now become a prize tourist destination. Hundreds of hotels host visitors

IO

eager for a quick dose of the sun. It was not always thus: when Massey bought his plot of land it was still a slice of desert, empty, isolated and wild – although it gives directly onto one of the longest, sandiest and most golden beaches of the Mediterranean. Massey's first friends here were Jean and Violet Henson, who had 'discovered' Tunisia in the 1930s. The Hensons were the catalysts who turned Hammamet into a social and artistic mecca before the war; several of their friends who had the means and savoir faire to enjoy it took houses here. The photographers Horst and Hoyningen-Huene took one, where they were hosts to Luchino Visconti and other luminaries. Elsa Schiaparelli then bought the house next door and the stage was set for a series of mad and marvellous adventures during the 1930s and 1940s. Like Horst and Huene before them, Massey and Berthelot designed a simple, almost cubic house based firmly on the forms of traditional Tunisian architecture. Only local materials and techniques were used. The main architectural element is the Tunisian *koubba* or 'sky-dome'. These whitewashed domes, which traditionally have four or eight sides, are an essential feature of the Tunisian landscape and can be found scattered all over the countryside. Massey's *koubba* tops the perfect cube of the living room, an example of form harmoniously adapted to function. The house was fashioned by the local mason, following Massey's brief for 'a seaside country home with donkeys, cows, dogs… plunked into nature, midst a wild garden'. Over thirty years later, his dream has mellowed beautifully. The graphic impact of the structure is as strong as ever, while successive layers of bright white limewash have softened the contours. The 'wild garden' has an avenue of trees, their trunks also painted white with lime, leading to a white basin which is heaven to plunge into on a scalding hot day. Beyond the white terraces, which are curtained off with cream toile to make outdoor living rooms, a footpath leads to the beach a few steps away. Called Dar el Qamar, or 'House of the Moon', it continues to evoke Hammamet's unique past.

David Massey

On the opening pages: a detail of the painted tile that indicates the entrance to the 'House of the Moon', and a portrait of the late Gaston Berthelot. *Left:* a view of the whitewashed platform giving onto the beach, which is reached by a palm-fringed path from the house. *Above:* a view of the *bassin* which holds spring water for watering the garden; it doubles as a natural swimming pool, with the limewashed steps serving as an improvized diving-board. All around is the exuberant Mediterranean vegetation that characterizes Massey's garden.

On these pages: the play of light and shade throughout the day adds to the dramatic impact of the typically Tunisian architecture. Although Massey designed the house himself he credits his Tunisian mason with improving the initial blueprints and sketches, instinctively modelling the local materials to create a modern take on age-old shapes and volumes. The *koubba*, below, the uneven limewashed walls and the lattice-work blinds, together with the cut-out stairs, are all elements that allow for great graphic impact, indeed the house was short-listed for the Aga Khan Architectural Prize in 1994.

Above: the bedroom on the top floor. The decoration here, with its colonial armchairs and Indian carpet, evokes Massey's many visits to India. The stone pillars are antique and were carved locally. *Opposite:* a corner of the outdoor terrace where Massey spends most of his time during the summer. To all intents and purposes this is the 'summer living room', tented off with elegant cream cotton drapes. Occasionally Massey entertains on a grand scale, with sumptuous dinners for *le tout Hammamet* in the garden pavilion. On more intimate occasions, friends are invited for cocktails on the terrace.

Hyères, the western frontier of the Côte d'Azur, was where foreigners with prim habits and starched clothes first began edging gingerly towards enjoyment at the edges of the Mediterranean. In the mid-nineteenth century it was a proud resort, a little inland perhaps, but with a view of the sea, frequented by aristocrats and socialites and embellished by an exotic newcomer – the palm tree – soon to become all the rage and a symbol of the nearby coast. Violets, figs and oranges were grown for colder lands as they had been centuries earlier for Versailles. In 1920 the novelist Edith Wharton bought the medieval monastery of Sainte Claire, and converted it into her last southern home. She wrote of it, 'I am thrilled to the spine. *Il y va de mon avenir*; and I fell as if I were going to get married – to the right man at last!' Another passionately conceived house of that period was the radical contemporary mansion built by Robert Mallet-Stevens for Marie-Laure and Charles de Noailles, patrons of the arts and modernists. It is one of the great architectural monuments on the Riviera, and the reason why many tourists visit Hyères today, although the town

II

has otherwise sunk into genteel decline. Its allure proved strong enough, however, to attract Frédéric Mechiche, Hyères' newest aesthete. When he arrived in the old quarter he was sceptical towards the charms of the well-preserved fourteenth-century alleyways and market square. Soon, however, he was convinced that 'some places in the world have an aura – things have happened here', evoking the quarter's illustrious and iconoclastic past residents. 'I have a horror of life on the Côte itself – because of the show-off element – but I love and respect the Mediterranean rhythm of life,' says Mechiche. 'I bought this house forty-eight hours after visiting it. Hyères is the perfect place for me. I can buy my croissants in an eighteenth-century boulangerie yet I'm only ten minutes from the airport and all the positive aspects of modernity. I bought the house across the street as well, in order to put up guests in comfort, so now I'm truly entrenched.' Mechiche is a well-known Parisian decorator whose signature style ranges from 1940s elegance to eighteenth-century prettiness – successfully applied to period architecture with a sense of theatre – and includes acres of distressed white or pastel walls. He has adopted a more gutsy take on his usual approach for his converted fishermen's and salt-gatherer's cottage, niched into the city's medieval ramparts. The fourteenth-century structure was re-done during the 1800s, but when Mechiche bought the place it had not been tampered with for a generation. The irregular walls, original plasterwork and ancient floors had not, therefore, all been disastrously modernized. He set to work to enhance that shabbiness, armed with the know-how of a professional. 'I like to feel the past on the walls, the lived-in aspect of the house – I have a horror of things too new or restored,' he says. While plastering the façade, for example, he mixed his ochre with mud and dirty water to give it that desirable murky look. If today the cottage looks deliciously decadent, it is thanks to Mechiche's ability to make terrific amounts of building work look as if they never happened. From an old photograph he worked out that certain windows had been bricked in and others enlarged, and set about recreating the originals. Then, taking his cue from a fragment of old paint under many more recent layers, he conjured up a weathered look with painstakingly tiny brush strokes. Mechiche also built a terrace on the top of the house, planted with jasmine and oleander that looks as if it has been there for centuries. Despite the romanticism of his decorating style, Mechiche adopts an utterly modern attitude to life in the house: no staff, because housekeeping and lots of cooking is part of the relaxed kind of holiday he favours; a gym in the basement, and everything delivered from the modern town that lurks up the road but seems a world away.

Frédéric Mechiche

On the opening pages: a portrait of Frédéric Mechiche, and a view of the roof terrace that was 'carved out like a slice of cake' to give him an outdoor spot. *Left:* a picture of the doorway, and, *below*, the graceful stairway as seen from the first-floor landing. The staircase was entirely reworked to give it a lightness that it had lost over the years. *Opposite:* the entrance hall with the pale olive walls that were painted and then repainted with tinted limewash. The table is a nineteenth-century garden piece, the chair is Biedermeier and has been painted by Mechiche.

On the previous double page: the dining room on the top floor. Mechiche inverted the traditional organization of these tall, thin village houses by putting the living room, dining room and kitchen on the top rather than the ground floor. The table is Louis XVI, in the *style Marie Antoinette au hameau* – a sophisticated take on the rustic. This, in contemporary terms, perfectly expresses Mechiche's own taste. The chairs are Provençal and Parisian, covered in white toile. The *pot à feu*, the period warming device standing against the wall, is neoclassical and stands on a Louis XVI column. The portrait is eighteenth-century English. *Below:* the fireplace, rebuilt with stones from the ground-floor chimney piece. The wall in watercolour trompe l'œil was painted by Mechiche. The chandelier is Gustavien. *Right:* a general view of the salon with its Louis XVI mirror and a rare 'Cresson' chair in front of it.

Below: a view from the salon in the tiny house across the road, which Mechiche bought on impulse in order to accommodate his guests. Its windows were reduced in size to respect the original eighteenth-century proportions. The side table – a trompe l'œil of books – is Empire, and the chair is Directoire. *Opposite:* a view of the nineteenth-century wrought-iron bed, now used as a sofa, that Mechiche has covered in fabrics from his own collection. The cushions are made out of linen bed sheets. The engravings are nineteenth century.

On the previous page: Mechiche created a fascinating library by enlarging the landing. In the foreground is the simple iron banister. The chair dates from the Restoration, while the small garden table is nineteenth century. The books are kept in happy disorder. *Opposite:* typical Provençal fare. One of Mechiche's great pleasures, while at Hyères, is shopping for the colourful local produce and preparing it himself. *Above:* the kitchen with its ancient stove, now converted to electricity. The stone sink dates from the eighteenth century.

Above: a corner of the bedroom showing candlesticks *au mercure* on a Louis XV Provençal table; the corner-piece is from the same period. The wrought-iron chandelier is eighteenth century. *Right:* the bathroom, in 'Tangiers colours' inspired by Matisse. *Opposite:* the bed, draped with rosy eighteenth-century *Toile de Jouy*. The chair is Louis XV. When Mechiche moved in, the bedroom was the most unspoilt room, with its little bedside cupboard still in place.

Opposite: a view of a quiet corner of one of the bedrooms in the guest house. Over the Directoire chair hangs an unusual travelling chandelier of the same period. The shelving is nineteenth century and made from simple planks. *Left:* the bed in the same room, with its *boutis* or traditional Provençal quilt. *Below:* the guest room on the ground floor in the main house, with Mechiche's signature bold stripes draped above the bed. Mechiche likes to think that his house looks rather like a fisherman's cottage where some hundred years ago an erudite traveller might have stayed and left a few good things behind – a whimsical yet apt description of the atmosphere.

The sea is green at Hammamet, and shallow, so that one has to stroll out to swim. It is particularly calm, perhaps reflecting the spirit of the Tunisians themselves – who seem the most Roman of the Arab races, the most tranquil, the most hedonistic. And it was the sea's haunting, seductive presence that in 1925 attracted Jean and Violet Henson to Hammamet. They came with dreams of Greece and Rome, of finding a new southern paradise, a background for their cultured and pleasure-seeking lives, an Athens in Africa. They were an unusual couple: he a demi-god of perfect masculine beauty, she a literary Englishwoman of that fragility that conceals great strength. They had known the Paris of the Dadaists; he had posed for Man Ray, met Cocteau, Bérard, Serge Lifar, she had travelled widely despite coming from the sheltered English elite. There was an extreme streak to these aesthetes, however, and together they dared to isolate themselves on the limewashed shores of Tunisia, spending the rest of their lives here. The Hensons' house was no summer residence for socialites but, quite simply, their home. They dug a garden

12

out of the sand and turned it into something legendary – the blueprint for all Mediterranean gardens – planted with all kinds of rare species. Whether brought from half a world away or from down the road, these plants all became irreversibly Mediterranean once they took root in Hammamet. Sweet water brought life; an *éolienne* (a wind-powered pump) was installed to extract water from deep under the ground and then splash it into a whitewashed *bassin*. (The *bassin* functions as both reservoir and swimming pool; here one floats for a moment in the delicious coldness when the body, feverish from the heat, has lost the very notion of cool, before taking delicious lemonade and orange-flower water at midday.) From here the precious stuff is designed to flow into the long canal, the main artery of the garden, and thence to the little rivulets which criss-cross it. The system was modelled on the most ancient mode of irrigation known to man, and still functions today. The Hensons built a low, white house with the archways and courtyards of Arabia, and filled it with the books and paintings of Europe. The world, as was fitting, came to them, and they entertained right across the cultures – on cushions, on the terraces, on the beach, in their legendary garden or in the double-height living room, always littered with the latest periodicals. Lamps by Giacometti, photographs by Horst, drawings by Christian Bérard and myriad other treasures would hang in the pale lilac hallway. At the same time Jean struck up deep friendships with the inscrutable Bedouins, whose horses he would water in times of drought. Together these complementary allegiances made the couple an intristic part of Hammamet. Today, Leïla Menchari is the devoted guardian of the flame and keeper of the Hensons' memory. An exotic Tunisian beauty, she is responsible for the theatrical window dressing of Hermès, the luxury Parisian boutique. She first met the Hensons as a child, on an errand for her mother, when she strayed into their garden seeking to deliver a message – 'my mother will not be coming to play cards this afternoon'. She got the wrong house, but fate had undoubtedly played the right card. Leïla, aged eight, brown-skinned, long-legged and on her summer holidays, was to become the Hensons' spiritual daughter. She was fascinated and receptive, absorbing all of their otherness, their Anglo-Saxoness, their passions. Years later, after Violet's death, Leïla watched over Jean. Every year, when Hermès unwillingly spares her for a month, Leïla Menchari spends the summer in the country of her birth and in her garden of adoption, battling with passion against the combined forces of nature and time, to keep the Hensons' Mediterranean dream alive.

Leïla Menchari

On the opening pages: a portrait of Leïla Menchari by Edouard Boubat. The detail shows the 'Garden of Venus', with its cactuses and mimosas. This view is of the stretch of garden next to the beach, where the heat presses down on you after bathing and before you reach the coolness of the ponds and the shady cyprus-planted alley leading to the house. *On the previous double page:* the neo-classical temple, built by the Hensons, at the end of a stretch of water studded with water lilies. *Opposite:* the mysterious inner courtyard, through which one enters the house. *Above:* the façade, with the chickens and peacocks that consider the garden their own.

On this page: two views of the corridor, painted a distinctive lavender tone. The trompe l'œil is by Jellel Ben Abdallah and disguises a cupboard door. *Opposite:* a view of the dining room alcove as seen from the drawing room, with its arched double-height ceiling. Most of the works of art are by friends of the Hensons. *On the following pages:* a view of the beach from the 'Garden of Venus', framed by stone columns. The columns were part of Violet and Jean's extensive collection of antiquities from Carthage and other Tunisian sites – even the cats had Punic gravestones at the Hensons.

On the opening pages: Caroline and Hans Neuendorf's daughter at play, and a view of the rooftop terrace of their family holiday home in Mallorca. The terrace is paved in the local Santanyi stone. *Right:* the approach to the house is along a white walkway comprising a flight of long, shallow steps with a sloping wall to the left. The house appears as a box, with only a mysterious slit for access. *Above:* the courtyard creates a striking entrance: after slipping through the slit in the high red wall the visitor emerges into this abstract space, an experience akin to stepping into a De Chirico painting. *Opposite:* The back wall is punctuated by a dramatic series of square windows, framing the views of the countryside beyond.

On the previous double page: a view of the shimmering 38-metre (125-foot) swimming pool. The solid block of the Neuendorf home is reflected in its waters. *On these pages:* different views of the pool, which protrudes theatrically into the olive groves, at right angles to the body of the house. The guest quarters and a garage are built underneath. At its tip the water descends into a children's pool, inspired by the constructions of Mexican architect Luis Barragán.

Opposite: a view from the kitchen-dining room towards the white path which leads to the house via the courtyard. The dense table in local stone was designed by Silvestrin. The chairs are by Hans Wegner. *Below:* another view of the same room showing the architects' ingenious 'double walls', designed to allow doors and windows, blinds and mosquito netting to be slid easily out of sight. This principal was applied throughout the house. *Left:* a corridor permits the master bedroom, dressing room and bathroom to enjoy privacy without actual doors.

Above and right: details of a perfectly minimalist bathroom. The stone sink was designed by Silvestrin in the shape of a baptismal font. The bath, inspired by traditional Japanese wooden tubs, is placed on the other side of a low wall in the local stone. The shower protrudes from the wall over a sloping floor which eliminates the necessity for a shower dish. *Opposite:* the midday sun illuminates the sensual texture of the bedroom's white walls. Both chairs are by Hans Wegner. Apart from the simple bed, the only other furniture is a long low shelf, which can also be used as a bench. All clutter and clothes are kept in the adjacent dressing room.

Surrounded by water, but always parched, Mallorca, the largest of the Balearic islands, features many of the elements that are considered quintessentially Mediterranean. The lofty ridges and deep ravines of its *serra* offer spectacular scenery, while the scrub that covers it is not unlike the fragrant Corsican *maquis* or the *garriguette* of southern France. The Moorish invasion brought the terracing which covers much of the fertile slopes; tomatoes, olives and carob are grown along with almonds, figs and apricots. A general Mediterranean reluctance to settle on the coast itself, from fear of raids by pirates, has meant that the oldest settlements and grand estates are situated inland – the convenience of being directly by the sea being sacrificed to safety. This house is a case in point, being over three hundred years old in parts, and set among rolling hills. A converted farm with thick walls daubed with limewash, and plaster stairs and banisters that have been worn by time into beautiful, undulating shapes, it is today one of Mallorca's grandest homes – despite having originally been built as a simple *finca*. Latterly it belonged to Chiquita Astor,

14

the Argentine-born socialite and *dame du monde*, who was one of the first of the island's aristocratic tenants. Her garden, which has been beautifully preserved, was designed by that Renaissance man *extraordinaire*, Cecil Beaton, and originally included a plantation of pampas grass to remind her of home. Today the property remains an adored holiday hideaway, and the old house continues to slumber serenely within earshot of the grazing goats. One of the most remarkable characteristics of the place is this very peace, the site being remarkably well protected from the bustle of island life, even in the height of the season. The serene proportions are most striking: it is a classical, L-shaped two-storey building with arches, vaulted porches and ancient wooden doors. Inside, the simplicity of the architecture has been respected, although the house has been beautifully fitted out under the energetic influence of Mimmi O'Connell. The dynamic London-based, Turin-born decorator jets off anywhere in the world that might require her cosmopolitan touch, and is particularly happy when transforming this kind of simple holiday structure. In this aged house she allowed herself to be guided by the rural character of the building. The interiors were kept white, and the rustic character of the walls and floors preserved. The new owners, who had promised Chiquita Astor that they would maintain the spirit of the place, are a young international couple. When they commissioned O'Connell they had already bought quantities of the local pottery for the kitchen cupboards and to be prettily adapted to use as sinks. They were hugely impressed with the way the designer whizzed round the place and created a comfortable, relaxed interior in under two months. The back door opens straight into the double kitchen which still has its original bread oven, beams and range – now adapted to a glittery iron and brass affair. Meals are taken either here or on one of the two patio terraces. On the ground floor there are local terracotta tiles underfoot, and upstairs the flooring is simple whitewashed plaster. The upstairs bedrooms have a somewhat monastic air; despite their creature comforts, they have been kept beautifully simple. Life here is lived outdoors, much as it must have been when the house was first built, with only the rosemary-scented breeze and grazing goats for company.

Mimmi O'Connell

On the previous pages: a portrait of Mimmi O'Connell, and a view of the façade of the typically Mallorcan farmhouse, known as a *posessió*. The ancient well can be seen in the foreground. *Opposite:* a corner of the garden, now mature and as pleasant as Beaton must have dreamed it all those years ago. *Above:* the front door, with its traditional sundial.

Opposite: a view of the traditional archway by the back door. The ground floor was probably once used for livestock and provisions, and this covered area would have been useful for storing tools and farming utensils. *Above:* the drawing room, a sophisticated take on country living. The sofas and armchairs were designed by O'Connell. *Left:* the undulating stairway that leads to the first floor. Leaning against the wall are O'Connell's signature decorative poles; these were inspired by an old, brightly coloured pole in a circus tent. The coat stand and chair are English Regency.

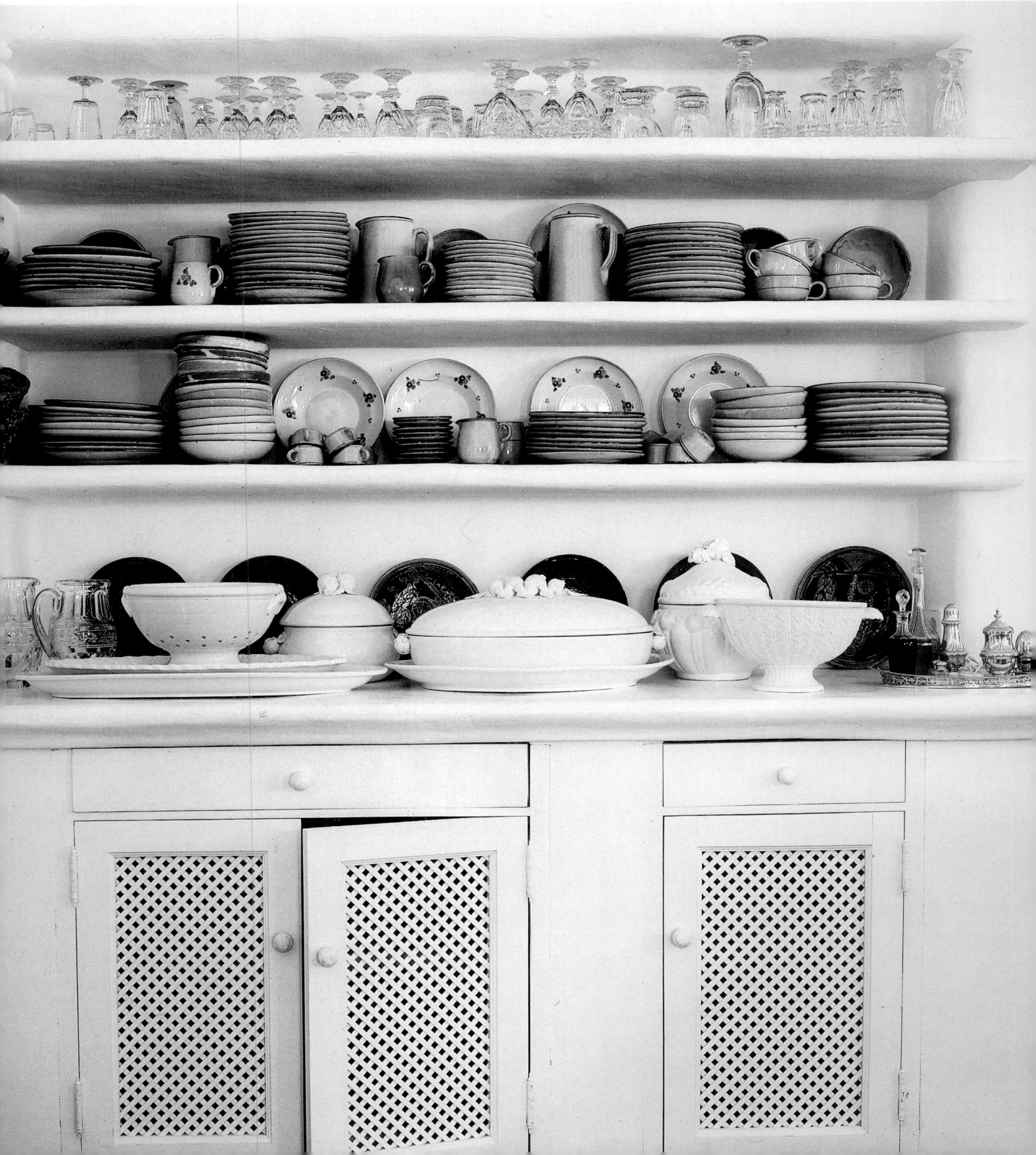

Opposite: a view of the corner of the kitchen used for storing flatware and glasses. The coloured ceramics are local and the white pieces are French. The lattice-work cupboard doors and the in-built shelf were at the house when O'Connell arrived, presumably installed by Chiquita Astor. *Above:* the ancient bread oven, now adapted for use as an open fire. The lanterns are part of a collection of eighteenth- and nineteenth-century pieces. The kitchen, which includes an ante-room, is large and spacious and is used as one of the main living spaces.

Above: an unusual sink made out a piece of the local ceramic ware and designed by the mistress of the house. *Right:* a view of the large master bedroom, under the eaves, showing the graceful English nineteenth-century iron bed. The all-white room features several touches of the wrought ironwork that is much used locally (although here the pieces were designed by Mimmi O'Connell), lending it a very Mediterranean feel. The luxurious white carpet is a handmade piece and was imported from Sardinia. In winter the fireplaces are kept lit, giving the bedroom a welcoming atmosphere.

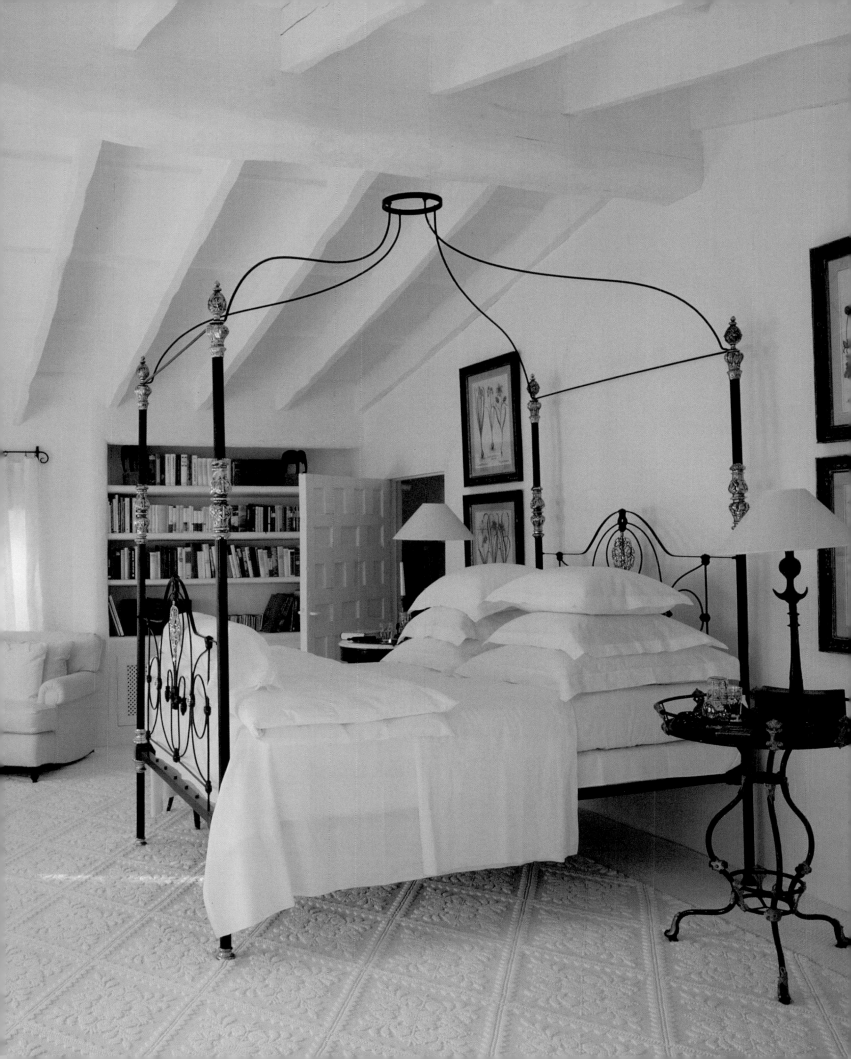

Elsa Peretti has one of those nomadic, multi-cultural lives that one can only envy: the world is her playground, her inspiration, her backdrop. Possibly today's most famous jewellery designer, Peretti was born in Florence – a particularly impermeable town, sealed up in its own splendour – and was educated in Rome and Switzerland. At twenty-one, with her coming of age, the door was opened onto the wide world. The minutiae of the Italian countryside, its pebbles, stones and vegetation, that she was to later to reproduce in her organic jewellery for Tiffany, were for the moment forgotten during a period of fruitful wandering through Asia and Europe. In the early 1960s she discovered Barcelona, a city fizzing with the repressed energy of the Fascist dictatorship. Here, to survive, she modelled for Salvador Dali and others, becoming something of a muse to the hedonistic intelligentsia known as the *gauche divine*. Barcelona gave Peretti a taste of freedom, as well as inspiration in the form of Gaudi's architecture and the natural beauty of the nearby Costa Brava. She was soon swept away to New York, but bought her first house, a ruin, in a small

15

abandoned Catalan village near Barcelona. In the early 1970s Peretti became a fixture of the New York scene as a model and design associate for the fashion designer Halston. She then joined Tiffany and Co., and ever since she has commuted between rural Spain and New York. Although Peretti is famous for her glamorous socializing and city life, her designs have always reflected the natural world: pebbles, beans, drops. In the USA she has won many awards and been honoured with a large-scale retrospective. Meanwhile in San Marti Vell, her Catalan hamlet, she has restored ten of the original houses, one of which is now the Elsa Peretti Foundation. She also has another Mediterranean home, but this is a very different hideaway: rural, secret and inaccessible. Peretti goes there often, to live simply, striding out with her sheepdogs on the blowy peninsula overlooking the sea, where the waves merge with the wind and the view has remained the same for centuries. This home is in her native Italy, near the Tuscan village of Porto Ercole, an hour and a half from Rome. It is a curious structure, a watchtower, situated at the end of a long and winding gravel track, with a bird's-eye view of the sea. Probably originally built in the thirteenth century as protection against the Moors, the square and spartan grey stone tower, popular as a nesting-site for vultures, was rebuilt in the sixteenth century by the Spaniards and was still used a hundred years ago for detecting marauders. Now, its soldiers' cells have been transformed into the epitome of comfort. The Torre l'Avoltore is the only one of her houses where Peretti has felt inclined to employ a decorator: her trusted Milanese friend Renzo Mongiardino. He swiftly realized that what Peretti wanted was a refuge, and that the building's hard lines and aggressive demeanour would need to be softened to make a comfortable retreat. Peretti had given him carte blanche, and Mongiardino took the decision to warm up the interior with a very theatrical approach. Recklessly he commissioned trompe l'œil frescoes of ruins and sky, as a way of bringing into the house all the blue sky that the slit windows had banished. The reception rooms are now perfectly cosy, with bright colour, painted walls and terracotta floors. The guest rooms are more simply stencilled in earthy tones, while the main fireplace takes the form of a monster with open mouth and shells in his hair – a surreal reference to Bomarzo, an organic sixteenth-century sculpture garden built by the Orsinis.

Elsa Peretti

On the opening pages: a portrait of Elsa Peretti, and a detail of the intricate tromp l'œil in her Italian home. This was painted to designs by the grand old man of Italian decorating, Renzo Mongiardino. *Opposite:* the outside dining table, Peretti's favourite spot. A perfect square made from chestnut wood, it has been worn grey by the weather. The view of Punta Argentario on the curving coast is virtually unspoilt. *Above:* a view of the façade of Torre l'Avoltore, built in local stone. The garden is carefully cultivated with fragrant Mediterranean scrub, including rosemary, thyme and myrtle. Peretti also owns extensive olive groves and vineyards, which are her pride and joy, for making her own oil and wine.

On the previous double page: a view of the beamed main living room. The fireplace is a rendering of the cave entrance in the Bomarzo, the Orsinis' sixteenth-century pleasure garden. The shells in the monster's hair are specimens that Peretti has collected over the years. It was carved in situ by one of Mongiardino's craftsmen. Of her friend who persuaded her to abandon the spartan look in favour of a delicious fantasy, Peretti says, 'He is not a decorator but someone who feels things.' The benches are upholstered in kilims, which are tough and can stand up to the dogs. The small table, with its carved nineteenth-century chairs, doubles as a dinner table. The stairs lead to the bedrooms on the second floor. *This page, left:* a detail of the trompe l'œil in the stairwell and the two living rooms. Full of neo-classical references, the theme is a kind of eternal Mediterranean romanticism. *Below:* the spiral stairway leads from a small salon on the top-floor landing to the terrace on the flat roof. Several coastal towns in Italy have preserved their flat-roofed buildings, which were built under Saracen influence. *Opposite:* a corner of the salon, showing a larger expanse of fresco. Adopting this technique, with all its rich detail, was an inspired idea to ensure that the tower would retain very little of its warrior-like atmosphere.

Opposite: a corner of the guest room favoured by Renzo Mongiardino when he comes to stay. The table was designed by Peretti around a piece of wood that she discovered in her father's oil refinery, thus providing a powerful link with the past. On the table is an extravagant piece of driftwood, found on the coast nearby. The minimalist chair was designed by a sculptor friend. *Left:* the bathroom of the main bedroom, with its terracotta tiles. *Below left:* a guest bathroom with an intricate cut-glass mirror and stencils. The sink was brought from Spain. *Below right:* the master bedroom with its library; of all her houses, Peretti considers this the one in which she reads the most. It is also the house where she most often goes for walks, finding much inspiration on her way.

At the edges of mainland Greece the land has been smashed into a thousand smithereens and randomly sown over the Aegean and Ionian seas, the blue womb of the Mediterranean civilization. The island of Spetsai, which lies so close to Athens that for centuries it has been regarded as a health-inducing sub-urb, often appears the least Hellenic of these thousands of splin-ters of land. Abundantly wooded, it was historically known as Pitouissa due to its natural growth of pines. Lawrence Durrell likened it to Corsica, or the Italian island of Ischia. Henry Miller loved it here, tak-ing greatly to its seraphic charms. Miller's discovery of Greece was profoundly significant for him, a spiritual experience which resulted in one of his most impor-tant books, *The Colossus of Maroussi.* No doubt the writer would have passed in front of this house, built in 1860 by one of the island's wealthy mariners, while unstrenuously swaying around the island in a local *fiacre* or horse-drawn carriage. (These carriages are still the only passenger vehicles to be allowed access to Spetsai Town, and their coachmen wield a considerable amount of local power.) As on

16

neighbouring Hydra, the island's prettiest houses were built by wealthy seafarers – buccaneers and merchants – in the eighteenth and nineteenth centuries, and are now protected by law. The architect Michael Photiadis has restored many of Spetsai's finest homes. This project was particularly close to his heart, however, since as a young man he was a frequent guest at the distinguished house. It was then the home of the American journalist Cyrus Schulzberger and his Greek wife Maria Landas. Photiadis, invited by their daughter, would be part of the rumbustious holiday crowd there. Schulzberger and his wife had met during the Second World War, where he was reporting and she was in the Resistance. Over the next two decades the place became known as a literary salon and a joyful holiday rendezvous. When the house was bought by an Athenian family in the early 1980s, Photiadis was faced with the task of restoring its original gracious volumes, which meant removing all of the hasty summertime additions which had been built on haphazardly. He also renovated the traditional large pebbled areas on the terraces and in the hanging gardens, and installed a staircase between the two main rooms (a kitchen-dining room and the salon above). These rooms look down onto the old port, through handsomely proportioned windows set into the thick walls of the austere façade. Glowing with colour and rich with decorative effects, they have high ceilings in painted wood. The mistress of the house, born into a family of collectors, has carefully furnished it with pieces that an eighteenth- or nineteenth-century captain could conceivably have brought back from his travels, a reference to the island's past. These include textiles, pictures and furniture, mostly Mediterranean and often with more charm than value. The tall rooms and the painted wooden floors with their wide planks provide a strong background against which the paintings, the oriental pieces and above all the collection of fish images work very well. She has respected the spirit of the old house but at the same time has completely redesigned the flora that surrounds it, visiting a large number of Mediterranean gardens to find inspiration. The terraces and garden have been replanted not only with the lavender and rosemary of the island, but also with English roses such as Constance Spry and Phillips Kitsgate.

Michael Photiadis

On the previous pages: a portrait of the architect Michael Photiadis, who restored this traditional large family home on the island of Spetsai; and a view of the patio façade of the house, showing the wrought-iron balustrade. The table, with its white marble top, was made locally. The chairs are the classic 'Butterfly' design from the late 1930s. *On this page and opposite:* views of the main salon on the first floor, which can be reached from the kitchen via a staircase installed by Photiadis. The nineteenth-century chandelier is Baltic, and the kilim is Shirvan, from the Caucasus.

On the previous pages: a view of the downstairs kitchen-dining room. The kitchen table is eighteenth-century French; the chairs come from a Greek café and are loved for their simple lines. Fish are a recurring motif, as can be seen in the collection of ceramics on the wall. *Opposite:* a local-style metal bed in one of the bedrooms. The white-painted wood and the thick exterior walls combine to lend a summery feel to the room. *Above:* Doric-style columns, made out of metal, line a pebbled walkway. *Right:* the same view seen through the entrance door.

On the opening pages: a portrait of Nicola del Roscio by Julian Schnabel, and a view of the patio with its flowering cherry tree dripping petals onto the nineteenth-century garden furniture. *Left:* a view from the *salone* through the bedroom, with its iron four-poster bed, from the 1700s, hung with cheerful Turkish fabric. The door frame, in silver leaf, is original to the house. *Opposite:* a view of the *salone* from its terrace. The door is also original, as of course are the superb eighteenth-century frescoes. The sofa is Empire, and the chairs are eighteenth-century – the square armchair and the pair by the window are Roman, the other pair are Venetian. Propped up against the walls are antique frames from del Roscio's superb collection.

Left: a detail of the multicoloured chapel, built for the resident cardinal in the eighteenth century. With its gilded saints and crosses, the look is very southern Italian. *Below:* a view of the dining table in the large vaulted kitchen. The chairs are British Arts and Crafts and the painting, *à la manière de Picasso*, is by Cy Twombly. *Opposite:* the incomparable view, showing Gaeta's two castles huddled together and overlooking the Mediterranean whence danger usually came. The Gulf of Gaeta is an ancient harbour steeped in history, and one of the most significant sites in southern Italy.

There is poetic justice in the fact that this aged *finca* should have fallen into the hands of Miguel Servera. For one thing he is passionately Mallorcan, and cares deeply about that island's singular heritage. That in itself makes him a fitting master for this farmhouse steeped in island history, with stones that are over a thousand years old. For another, he is a man of the arts who might well have become a full-time architect had his life not taken another turn. As it is, he busies himself with architecture and building restoration whenever time allows. His projects look outwards, not inwards, towards the Mediterranean as a whole – they could be adapted for anywhere on these coasts. This attitude is perfectly in keeping with the heterogeneous history of this house, which was presented by the Spanish king to an Arab family as payment for services rendered. And finally, there even exists an obscure blood-tie. Although Servera came across the house by chance, he later discovered that one of his great-grandmothers had been related to the original family who owned the property and lived there for hundreds of years. When not engaged in architectural

18

activities, Servera spends much of his time running an art gallery which features such painters as Saura and Eduardo Chillida. His was the first gallery to exhibit the internationally acclaimed young Mallorcan painter, Miquel Barceló. The gallery is considered the most innovative on the island, but modestly takes its name from the street: Sa Aleta Frida. It opens during the summer months, when the island throbs with international visitors. The walls of Servera's solid *finca*, hung with modern art, reflect the interests of the man who was the first director of the nearby Joan and Pilar Miró Foundation, Mallorca's leading centre for the arts and a living expression of Miró's desire for a living space open to all culture. Servera's house – which was originally surrounded by a vast tract of land – had always been used as a farmhouse, although for much of its history it was lived in by labourers rather than the owner of the farm. Much of the building was used for storing grain; the men would congregate in the arched hall

and the adjoining kitchen for warmth. The building comprises an unusual combination of different architectural elements, and Servera did a great deal of restoration work on it, but with such a delicate touch that few would guess at the months of re-structuring involved. It probably grew out of a tower-like structure, built for defence, before being transformed into the Arab *alqueria*. It was then lived in by the same family for over six hundred years. The 150 hectares (37,000 acres) of land that Servera owns today were a thousand in those days, but much the same products were grown: wheat, olives, grapes. The house still has its own mill and wine and oil press, situated in the wings as is the custom. It was built to the traditional *Mallorquin* pattern, in solid stone with limewashed interiors and following a c-shaped plan, with doors and windows often aligned to give the impression of transparency. Servera lives in his house with the serenity of someone who knows that things are as they should be in the heart of his beloved island, and that his *finca* is harmoniously living her thousandth year within a context that has changed surprisingly little.

Miguel Servera

On the previous pages: a portrait of Miguel Servera, and a view of the façade of his Mallorcan *finca*, which is essentially seventeenth-century but with a thirteenth-century arched doorway. *Opposite:* a view of the outbuildings in one of the wings. The patio is planted with bougainvillaea and geraniums, the trees are the local *encinas*. The window with the iron grille is that of the *finca*'s chapel. *Above:* view of the garden, which has a large cistern that collects rainwater to keep the vegetation luxuriant. The porch trellis is planted with local vines for shade, and the iron furniture is nineteenth-century Mallorcan.

Below: a detail of the larder, hung with typical local *charcuteria* and bounty from the garden. *Opposite:* the grand hall, medieval in its proportions, is the heart of the house. The long wooden bench has been there 'forever'; it is probably six-teenth- or seventeenth-century. The sheepskins that cover it are similar to those that the workmen would have used when the house was a home for the farm's labourers.

Above: a detail of the master bedroom with its heavy Mallorcan four-poster bed in mulberry wood. It is hung with the fine cotton embroidery that is one of Mallorca's most traditional crafts. The detail shows a small writing desk in one of the guest rooms. The painting above the desk is an early piece, from 1977, by Miquel Barceló. Servera recalls how he rooted it out of the tempestuous young painter's wastepaper basket, guessing that he was on the path to greatness. *Opposite:* a walled-in alcove typical of the local style, containing an eighteenth-century iron bed. The vegetable-fibre carpet is also local, in a design known as *de pleita*. The embroidered curtain is nineteenth-century, as is the embroidered folding chair.

Franca Squarciapino and Ezio Frigerio are part of the contemporary theatre world's elite. Over the last decade their names have been linked with some of the most significant productions of the European stage, and close collaborations with directors such as the Italian Giorgio Strelher or the Catalan Josep Maria Flotas have led them to create a new aesthetic world, challenging the accepted boundaries of stage drama. Frigerio is a gifted set designer, an expert in creating that essential quality of all theatre, the suspension of disbelief, and drawing the audience into a play. Squarciarpino has won several awards (including an Oscar) for her film costumes, and often works with Frigerio on theatre productions. Over ten years ago the Italian couple took a radical lifestyle decision: they would be based partly in Paris, whose central location and atmosphere pleased them, and for the rest of the year on a wild and isolated strip of the Turkish coast near Izmir, where life was cheaper and more pleasant. Thus, every six or seven months they pack up their central Paris workshop and studio and, together with their assistants, transport their theatrical universe to

19

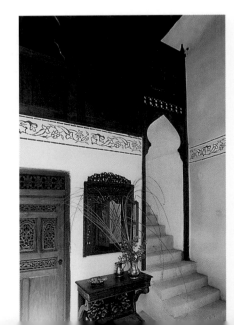

the Mediterranean atmosphere of the Turkish coast. The assistants' partners and children are always invited too, so the amber stone house by the sea becomes a kind of bustling commune with plenty of guests coming to stay and a large amount of creative work getting done in a charmingly cheerful manner. From May to September everyone enjoys the steady good weather, the extraordinary views and the unhurried pace of life that the house, constructed from scratch according to Frigerio's own blueprint, affords. 'The house was built by a group of 36 Anatolian workmen that we had recruited in the hinterlands. According to ancient customs, they farm in the summer and build – mostly mosques – in the winter. They arrived in a rackety old bus and set up camp in big white tents. My architect, the Russian Alexander Beliaev, moved in with them. It looked and felt for all the world like a medieval construction site. After exactly one hundred days they got back on their bus and left. The house was finished.' Frigerio, who studied architecture, delights in telling this story. 'In Italy we make such a fuss about building. It's so different here. The cupola over the living room, for instance, was built by ordinary workmen with no internal reinforcements or complicated calculations. It was quite incredible.' The house has been conceived along the lines of what he calls 'an occidental take on the exotic: pure orientalism, the East as perceived through the eyes of a European.' As it was designed for summer living there are no internal corridors, only exterior walkways that allow marvellous glimpses of sea, beach or landscape as you move around the house. The decorating process required a degree of initiative. For various reasons, many of the skilled artisan-carvers – who traditionally had often been Jews, Armenians or Greeks – had emigrated. After some research, Frigerio decided that the traditional woodwork that is so striking in the traditional Turkish *yallis*, and with which he wanted to structure his interior, would have to come from elsewhere. He chose Indonesia, a reputed source of Islamic carving and a country that once had strong cultural ties with Turkey. A trip or two resulted in his commissioning the magnificent woodwork that is a key feature of the house. Made from teak, it is highly resistant to the salt and humidity that comes from the beach – which is situated only a few steps away from the front door.

Franca Squarciapino
& Ezio Frigerio

On the opening pages: a detail of the inside stairway, showing the harmonious combination of plaster, carved wood and stone; the detail shows a segment of the wild and deserted Turkish coast. *Opposite:* three exterior details of the virtuoso stone carving executed by Anatolian builders. The house belies its recent construction; the use of local materials means that it has successfully blended into its surroundings. *Above:* the curved walls of the wing containing the sitting room. The two cupolas reflect the local mosque-inspired architecture.

Opposite: a view of the spectacular full-length carved wooden screens from Indonesia. Behind them are French windows which lead out from the sitting room onto the terrace. *Above:* the French windows seen from the exterior, showing the dramatic arches and stone banding. *Left:* rounded arches give onto a stone-flagged walkway. The house has no interior corridors; instead, family and guests – who only really use the house in summer – use these walkways as a means to get from one room to another.

Above and opposite: two views of the sitting room. The intricate wooden furniture and the screens were all hand-carved in Indonesia, a country with strong cultural ties to Turkey. (Frigerio was amused to find that even the national form of theatre in Turkey was inspired by Indonesia's traditional shadow theatre.) The room boasts a pretty perspective of the garden. *On the following double page:* a view of the convivial kitchen with its arched ceilings, long wooden table and plaster fireplace. The hand-painted tiles are local and add to the Mediterranean atmosphere of the room.

Below and opposite: views of two of the bedrooms. The rooms have been designed to be as cool as possible, with thick stone walls, screens against the sun and windows open to the sea breezes. The stone-flagged floors and white plaster walls and balustrades add to the Mediterranean feel. The overall impression is colonial and orientalist, with a modern twist. The wooden screens and furniture have been imported from Indonesia, a country whose artisans work in a similar way to the Turkish craftsmen of the past.

Yvonne Sursock, Lady Cochrane, lives in her natal Palais Sursock, without doubt the most beautiful house in the Lebanon. It is the kind of palace that orientalist dreams are made of, with tall slender columns, filigree stonework, wide sweeps of Italianate marble stairs and glorious views of the Mediterranean. The grand entrance may now be somewhat littered with rubble, and a bathroom mirror smashed by a bullet hole, but the Sursock palace still stands proudly in the centre of Beirut, just as it did when it was built by Lady Cochrane's grandfather in the 1860s. The plain exterior gives little away, but inside is a unique hybrid of the Scottish baronial style with Arab and Florentine influences. This was one of several Sursock family homes built two or three generations ago along the cluster of Beirut avenues bearing their name. The Sursocks are an ancient clan who originated in Byzantine times; this particular branch were Greek Orthodox from southern Turkey, and made their fortune largely from investing in the Suez Canal. The Palais Sursock was built as a fitting home for that eminent family, who were then known as 'the

20

Rothschilds of the East'. Up until the 1960s, when Beirut still deserved its own nickname of 'the Paris of the Orient' and every diplomat hoped to be posted there, the house rang with laughter, parties were held at a feverish pace, and big cars purred up to the gates depositing guests under the jacaranda trees. In retrospect, of course, those good times were doomed, full of the poignancy of the last fine days before the storm which marks the end of summer. Politics began to taint the dream, and with the bomb that was to be the first of many, the party was over forever. So much has been destroyed in Beirut that the past is gone without a hope of being re-lived. In Lady Cochrane's words, her home is 'a house full of memories'. Her children are now grown up and her husband, the Irish baronet Sir Desmond Cochrane, died in 1977. A fervent supporter of Lebanese architecture, Lady Cochrane is a radical denouncer of the modern atrocities that are being thrown up seem-

ingly at random in the campaign to rebuild the Lebanon. A scholar of what she calls the Lebanese 'genius for using stone sensibly and decoratively', she is a remarkable woman who evokes the glamour of a very different past. Likewise, the Palais Sursock remains one of the handful of grand Mediterranean residences that epitomize a long-gone palatial way of life. However, the theme of this book is not houses of monumental historical importance but those of more modest construction. Shown on these pages, therefore, is a pleasure pavilion and guest house nestled in the heart of the Palais Sursock's luxuriant garden. It was first built as the turkish bath of the main residence but has subsequently been transformed into what is rather charmingly known as the *kiosque des visiteurs*. The walls are eighteenth-century wooden panels, carved and inlaid by Syrian craftsmen, and the interior evokes a past life as the family's own *hammam*. Here, in the midst of the garden, history seems to stand still; one can almost hear the tinkle of the piano from the grand salon in the big house, as if Beirut had never been destroyed.

Yvonne Sursock, Lady Cochrane

On the opening pages: an exterior view and detail of the *hammam* building in the gardens of Sursock Palace. *Above:* a view showing the greenhouse-like atmosphere of the guest pavilion. In this clement country the barriers between inside and out are often blurred. Niched in the heart of the garden, the building is surrounded by exuberant greenery, its large windows letting in both light and plants. *Right:* the precious fabrics and furniture in the *hammam* come from throughout the Middle East.

On these pages: A stucco-type finish, traditional for buildings that have to withstand humidity, has been used for the walls. It has been applied in bands for strong graphic effect. The fountain is typical of the region, as are the arched ceilings and corridors. The dining room, with its polished mahogany table, has a definite English feel to it.

Right: the bedroom, glimpsed through the traditional heavy *hammam* door. *Below:* the bathroom, with its impressive stained-glass window, which provides a central focus. The baroque inlaid pieces are Syrian. *Opposite:* despite the chocolate-box proportions of the *hammam*, the impressively high windows give a sense of grandeur to the whole. Throughout, the decoration is based on oriental pieces with touches of a very English nineteenth-century aesthetic. The result is extremely elegant.

The Vallois' gallery of Art Deco furniture on the rue de Seine in Paris is one of the city's more confidential addresses, its vast spaces studded with polished pieces by the grand masters of the genre such as Ruhlmann, Dunand and Printz. The Vallois opened up shop in the centre of the left bank's tangle of streets in 1971, specializing in 'only the best pieces' of Art Deco. They had begun their business in a rather more modest gallery on the *route nationale* that runs between Monte Carlo and the Cap d'Ail, a corner of the Côte d'Azur that has maintained much of its old charm and still has several Edwardian villas. Cheska Vallois remembers going for long walks and looking wistfully through the palm trees to the mansions that looked like oversized cream cakes, with their balustrades and balconies suspended over the sea, still as glamorous as in the Riviera's heyday. They belonged to an era when society would spend the winter here, when Queen Victoria visited and when the poet and journalist Liégard wrote a forgettable book with a an unforgettable title – *La Côte d'Azur* – finally conjuring up a name for the hitherto unchristened coastline between

21

Hyères and Menton. After the success of his 1887 publication Liégard married an heiress who inherited a villa in Cannes, called 'Les Violettes'. Just over a hundred years later, the Vallois bought a turn-of-the-century villa with the very same name on the extremity of Cap d'Ail, 'with a 360° view of the sea'. The house was sadly neglected, having belonged to two English sisters who could not agree which of them should inherit the parental property. But the terraces jutting out over the sea were still there, as were the French windows, high ceilings, the ornamental balustrade and the gracious proportions. 'Les Violettes' is the epitome of a certain Mediterranean style that flourished on the Riviera when the industries of escape and illusion first became fashionable. These were the holiday homes of people who never worked. The Vallois not only took up the task of restoration but also extensively replanted the dying garden, putting in palms and Mediterranean shrubs that could resist the climate and the sea air. In their 1,200 square metres (1,400 square yards) of land they also decided to build a swimming pool. After careful consideration it was set on the roof of a one-storey extension. The flamboyant result is perfectly in keeping with the ornate lines of the Edwardian mansion. Blue swimming pool and azure sea form one uninterrupted line of vision, adding a Hollywood-style allure to the garden. When they turned to decorating the interior, the Vallois were faced with a dilemma: the shagreen, straw marquetry and lacquer of the sophisticated furniture that they specialize in would have quickly degenerated in the salty air. They decided to opt for the light-hearted whimsy of pure 1940s style – plaster, raffia, wood, wrought iron – mixed with some contemporary pieces such as those by Garouste and Bonetti, and the art of the Ecole de Nice, to which Bob Vallois, as a native of the Côte d'Azur, is particularly attached. The impetus for the blue and white look that dominates the interior came from the tiled floor; with its classic Riviera colours, it plays with the barriers between inside and out.

Cheska & Bob Vallois

On the opening pages: portraits of Bob and Cheska Vallois and a view of the terrace of their holiday home on the Cap d'Ail peninsula. *On the previous double page:* a spectacular view of the swimming pool and the specially constructed terrace. *On these pages:* views of the exterior and the garden. The palette was determined by the Mediterranean itself, which also dictated the planting of the garden. The balustrade, left, had once boasted unusual blue ceramic mouldings. of which only one baluster survived. The Vallois used this as a model for restoring the rest. The garden table and chairs in cement, below, with a tromp l'œil tree-bark pattern, were found in Paris and are probably early 1940s.

Above: a 1940s Serge Roche sconce in plaster, from the Paris antique dealer Christian Sapet, part of the pair that helped decide the spirit of the interior. The high-backed dining chairs are by Jean-Charles Moreux. *Opposite:* locally made wartime armchairs and sofa, in plaited cord, in the salon. The room's original hand-painted ceilings have been carefully restored. The pair of lamps are by Garouste and Bonetti, the ottoman in the alcove is by Serge Roche.

Opposite: a visitors' bedroom, with a plaited plaster lamp and a console by Serge Roche. The sconces are plaster and the curtains, in hard blue, are by Shyam Ahuja. *Above:* the 'African' bedroom, 'a pretty room filled with things of no particular distinction'. *Right:* a guest bedroom with a contemporary lamp by Ingo Maurer and white iron furniture by Garouste and Bonetti, whose light lines echo the 1940s feel of the rest of the furniture.

Dimiti Xanthoulis lives at the foot of the Acropolis, overlooking the church of St Nicholas, in a unpretentiously workaday quarter of Athens, hard by the flea market. The building is 1930s, and used to house an important collection of Greek folk art before it was moved to more glamorous quarters in Plaka, the Athens equivalent of Paris's Latin quarter. Xanthoulis is happy in his old-fashioned neighbourhood, which manages to remain relatively protected from the chaos of modern-day Athens. Moreover, he loves his chirpy little flat, which is smaller than what he has been used to but consequently enviably easy to maintain. As an antique dealer specializing in the arts of Asia, he is often away travelling and recognizes that the small flat is perfect for his needs. But just occasionally, and despite the fact that he claims no longer to deserve his reputation as a 'man about town', he recklessly squeezes up to sixty people in his flat for buffet dinners – which, in his own words, 'makes the atmosphere instantly festive'. His main regret is that he can only enjoy a pocket-handkerchief-sized terrace – the Greek summers beg outdoor living.

22

Although Xanthoulis emphatically denies decorating as such, the atmosphere in the house speaks volumes for his natural feeling for colour and proportion. The strong Mediterranean palette was improvized, taking its cue from the traces of previous coats of paint found peeling beneath the old wallpaper. In the drawing room, however, the distressed walls that were revealed had such a chromatic impact that he simply left them that way. The unusual bits and pieces that are the fruits of Xanthoulis's wanderings in Asia also lend the flat much of its character. 'Juxtaposing so many objects from different cultures goes back to the old Mediterranean tradition of travelling around the rim of the world – for at one time that sea was the whole world – and collecting things from other lands.' Xanthoulis spent the wild 1970s in Paris, experiencing the freedom of the gay revolution and the delights of the intellectual underground, where he was close to such luminaries as Louis Aragon and Marguerite Duras. He moved back to his native Greece in 1983, disillusioned with the frivolities of his artist's life – despite the fact that his work had been displayed at galleries in Paris and New York. He began to dabble in the ancient art of Turkey, his ancestral home. This dual allegiance to Greece and to

Turkey – two great countries which have so often been at cultural, religious and, most of all, territorial loggerheads – stimulated his interest in all traces of the Ottoman Empire, and consequently in Arabian and north African arts. India provided another powerful source of antiques, and in due course he began to specialize in Asia as a whole. Nowadays, if Xanthoulis is not in his blue world of books and beauty you might well run across him at cocktails at the Strand hotel in Rangoon, or the Imperial in Dehli, obeying, he says, that Mediterranean impulse for exploration.

Dimitrios Xanthoulis

On the opening pages: a portrait of Dimitri Xanthoulis and a detail of the tiny but idyllic terrace in his Athens flat. *Opposite:* a colonial-style chair, from Sri Lanka; the sconce, also reproduced in the detail, is nineteenth-century Argentine. The portrait of Xanthoulis is by Dimitri Papaioannou. *Below:* a wall sculpture by Nina Papa hangs in the living room. The vase is nineteenth-century Japanese, the lamp and table both 1950s.

Above: in the bedroom is a Dutch nineteenth-century four-poster covered with a Sussani fabric from Uzbekistan. The round table, with elaborately carved feet, is Sri Lankan, and the chandelier is Italian. *Right:* a baroque Catholic altar from the south of India, part of Xanthoulis's collection of religious and emblematic pieces from Asia. *Opposite:* the intensely azure corridor. The shelves, for paperbacks, successfully play on perspective and give a focal point.

Opposite: the dining room, with a fine Greek bookcase in walnut. Ceramic pieces from Central America and Pakistan are displayed here and on the table. The chairs were designed by the atelier of Walter Gropius for the American embassy in Athens, probably in the late 1950s. *Above:* the kitchen is decorated with murals by Papaioannou, inspired by comic strips. *Right:* cookbooks and prints in the kitchen, with a typically Spanish oil pourer. The room has the same warm atmosphere as the rest of the house.

This book has been put together with the help and support of my assistants Anna Davenport, Anna Vidal, Sophie Djerlal and Marianne Chedid.

Jean Pierre Godeaut was a constant source of fantastic images and ideas, and Karen Howes was as usual extremely helpful.

A big thank you to my agent Maggie Philips at Ed Victor, for her part in the proceedings.

This book is dedicated to my Mediterranean family: Sabrina, Louisa, Gustav and Enrique, and to my mother whose love of these shores caused me to be born on them.

Berger, Hans Georg and Hervé Guibert. *Lettres d'Egypte*. (Actes Sud, 1995.)

Blume, Mary. *Côte d'Azur: Inventing the French Riviera*. (Thames and Hudson, 1994.)

Boyd, Alastair. *The Road from Ronda*. (Collins, 1969.)

Bradford, Ernle. *Ulysses Found*. (Sphere, 1967.)

Brenan, Gerald. *The Face of Spain*. (Penguin Books, 1966.)

Duncan, Paul. *Discovering the Hill Towns of Italy*. (Potter, 1990.)

Durrell, Lawrence. *The Greek Islands*. (Book Club Associates, 1978.)

—. *Bitter Lemons*. (Faber and Faber, 1967.)

—. *Reflections on a Marine Venus*. (Faber and Faber, 1963.)

—. *Spirit of Place*. (Faber and Faber, 1969.)

Finlayson, Iain. *Tangier: City of the Dream*. (Flamingo, 1993.)

Goldfinger, Myron. *Arquitectura Popular Mediterránea*. (Gustavo Gili, 1993.)

Guerber, H.A. *Greece and Rome*. (Myths and Legends, 1994.)

James, Henry. *A Little Tour in France*. (Penguin Travel Library, 1985; orig. pub. 1884.)

Jong, Erica. *The Devil at Large: On Henry Miller*. (Chatto and Windus, 1993.)

Lawrence, D.H. *Sea and Sardinia*. (Olive Press, 1923.)

Leigh Fermor, Patrick. *Mani: Travels in the Southern Peloponnese*. (Penguin Books, 1984.)

Miller, Henry. *The Colossus of Maroussi*. (Minerva, 1991; orig. pub. 1941.)

Montalbán, Manuel Vázquez. *Barcelonas*. (Verso, 1992.)

Morris, Jan (ed.). *Travels with Virginia Woolf*. (Pimlico Press, 1997.)

Munthe, Axel. *The Story of San Michel*. (Flamingo Modern Classics, 1995.)

Newby, Eric. *On the Shores of the Mediterranean*. (Harvill, 1984.)

O'Faolain, Sean. *A Summer in Italy*. (Eyre and Spottiswoode, 1949.)

Stark, Freya. *The Journey's Echo*. (Harvey, 1963.)

Theroux, Paul. *The Pillars of Hercules*. (Penguin Books, 1995.)

Walker, D.S. *The Mediterranean Lands*. (Methuen, 1960.)

Wharton, Edith. *A Backward Glance: An Autobiography*. (Everyman, 1993; orig. pub. 1934.)

Waugh, Evelyn. *Labels*. (Penguin Twentieth-Century Classics, 1985; orig. pub. 1930.)